I Like
Being
Catholic

I Like

Being

Catholic

Treasured Traditions,
Rituals, and Stories

Edited by

Michael Leach and

Therese J. Borchard

DOUBLEDAY

New York   London   Toronto   Sydney   Auckland

PUBLISHED BY DOUBLEDAY
a division of Random House, Inc.
1540 Broadway, New York, New York 10036

DOUBLEDAY and the portrayal of an anchor with a dolphin are trademarks
of Doubleday, a division of Random House, Inc.

Pages 157–59 consist of an extension of this copyright page.

Book design by Donna Sinisgalli

Library of Congress Cataloging-in-Publication Data

I like being Catholic / edited by Michael Leach and Therese J. Borchard.— 1st ed.
p.   cm.
1. Catholic Church.   2. Catholics.   I. Leach, Michael, 1940–
II. Borchard, Therese Johnson.
BX885 .I2 2000
282—dc21   00-038424
ISBN 0-385-49951-5

First Edition

October 2000

1   3   5   7   9   10   8   6   4   2

CONTENTS

Contents

Contents

FOR
OUR TEACHERS

❦

I LIKE BEING CATHOLIC

What do Martin Scorsese, Cokie Roberts, William F. Buckley, and other famous people have in common with 63 million ordinary folk across the U.S.A.? They share a deep affection for some of the treasured traditions, rituals, and stories that run through the bloodstream of American Catholics. And they celebrate them in this book.

The title comes from a memorable answer given by Andrew Greeley on the *Donahue* show. A woman in the audience scolded him, "If you don't like the Catholic Church, why don't you stop being a priest and leave the church?" His spontaneous response: "I *like* being Catholic!"

The people who contributed to this book like being Catholic.

They may not always agree with the Church's rules but they wouldn't think of being anything else. Catholicism is in their bones.

They may find other Catholics too liberal or too conservative but they will always give them the kiss of peace. Catholicism is in their hearts.

They may call themselves lapsed Catholics or recovering Catholics or good-enough Catholics but they are always on the lookout for what is good and beautiful and true. Catholicism is in their eyes.

And it never goes away.

Being a Catholic is about seeing what's really there. It's about a baby whose Father's house has many mansions but who chooses to be born in a manger. It's about the cardboard stable and plaster figures we put beneath the Christmas tree. It's about symbols that remind us of what is real. Being a Catholic is about seeing the things that last.

It's also about people and stories and memories. Like Martin Scorsese, many Catholics are grateful for the Sisters who wrapped their knuckles but also built their self-esteem. Their faith is embodied in grandparents and godparents, in the sagas of saints and the rumors of angels. They remember the touch of a medal on their chest, the smell of incense smoking from a thurible, the midnight glow of Easter candles that really were a thousand points of light. Novels and movies and songs remind them of spiritual truths long buried or newly learned. The word Catholic is more to them than the answer to a census question; it is acknowledgment of the Word that was impressed on their hearts before they began to beat.

This is not a book of theology. It is simply about the good things that come with being Catholic. It is about what Teilhard de Chardin called "the chosen part of things." It endeavors to show, in word and picture, with pride and joy, why so many of us *like* being Catholic.

Michael Leach and Therese J. Borchard
January 2000

Chapter One

IT'S FUN TO BE CATHOLIC

BY ANDREW M. GREELEY

In its best moments Catholicism is the happiest of the major world religions. It is permeated by the reverent joy of Christmas night, the exultant joy of Easter morn, the gentle joy of First Communion, the satisfied joy of grammar school graduation, the hopeful joy of a funeral mass, the confident joy of a May crowning. Catholicism is shaped by the happiness of hymns like *O Come Emmanuel, Adeste Fideles,* the *Exultet,* and *Bring Flowers of the Rarest.*

Catholicism is an old, variegated, complex religious heritage. Many different cultural streams have emptied into its vast rivers. New ones still pour into it today. One can find in its history almost anything one wants—superstition, ignorance, bigotry, cruelty, arrogance, pride. One can easily find such realities today, too. Our ancestors have tortured and burned heretics and witches. They have murdered pagans, Muslims, Jews, Greeks, Protestants, and other Catholics. Anyone who has been raised Catholic has had ex-

perience with the harsh, negative, dour, repressive components of our heritage. Yet at its best—and all religions should be judged by their best—Catholicism is essentially a religion of sacramentality and community, a religion which believes that God is everywhere in our daily life and world and that we honor God as part of a community of believers. Anglican historian Owen Chadwick, in his book *The Popes and European Revolution*, comments, "The religious world of Haydn and Mozart had this characteristic of the Catholic eighteenth century, that it was a world of happy religion. . . . Like rococo architects, these were not men of an otherworldly religion, or (if they were) the other world was close to this world and permeated all its being."

Precisely. Perhaps without realizing it Professor Chadwick put his finger on the essence, the genius, the fundamental orientation of Catholicism, that aspect of our heritage which distinguishes us from all the other great world religions. We believe that the sacred is everywhere, that it lurks among us, sanctifying everything. We live in haunted houses, enchanted by the Holy Spirit. God is not (only) distant. God is among us in the water, the bread and the wine, the oil, the body of the beloved. And in the

Andrew Greeley, 1928: a sociologist contemplates the future

sun and the moon and the stars, in reconciliation after quarrels, in the touch of a friendly hand, in a glorious summer sunrise, in a chill winter sunset behind a frozen lake, in a familiar face seen in a crowd after many years of absence, in the cool waters of summer and the blazing fire of winter, in chocolate ice cream (with raspberry sauce!), in a joyous romp with our lover. Grace is everywhere. All is grace!

Alone of the major world religions, Catholicism affirms life, affirms flesh, affirms pleasure, affirms art and music, affirms a God who is present in the objects and events and persons of daily life. Hence we have angels and saints and souls in purgatory and stained glass and statues and Mary the Mother of Jesus. They all remind us of the presence of God in the Sacraments as well as in all the sacraments of our world.

Sure, Catholicism can easily slip over into superstition, folk religion, and a syncretistic blend with paganism. But other world religions that emphasize the distance of God and the god-forsaken nature of our world risk reducing the world to an empty and almost meaningless place. God is both present and absent, of course, both near and far, both immanent and transcendent. Catholicism bets that its emphasis on his presence, his nearness, his immanence, is legitimated by the mystery of the incarnation, that the word became flesh and dwelt among us (literally pitched his tent among us).

This appeal, this attractiveness, this charm of Catholicism is the reason why we remain Catholic, no matter the sins of the past or the foolishness of the present. Once a Catholic, it is said, always a Catholic. If Catholicism can enchant and enthrall your imagination in the early years of your life, you will always be haunted by it. As novelist Alice McDermott said, with considerable pride, we are forever doomed to be Catholic. There's no turning back.

Somehow too many of our teachers and our leaders don't seem to understand that we remain Catholic and always will be Catholic because of stories of the presence of grace in the world, stories of God's love all around us. Most Catholics know better. They know with St. Therese of the Infant Jesus (and the Holy Face) that God is nothing but mercy and love. They know with the Irish Dominican poet Paul Murray that God loves us so much that if any one of us should cease to exist He would die of sadness. They know with the American (and Chicago) theologian Robert Barron that God cannot help but love us with all the tender love of a mother.

There is a distinctively Catholic imagination—sacramental, liturgical, analogical, call it what you wish—which enables Catholics to see the world through a different set of lenses. That is the first reason it is fun to be Catholic.

Catholicism is thus a religion of festivity and celebration, of holidays and parties, of a sacred calendar, of Christmas cribs and Easter lilies, of processions and pilgrimages, of seasons and colors, of special prayers and special patrons. They are all part of the explanation of why Catholicism is a happy religion and why it is fun to be Catholic.

Andrew Greeley, 1938: a future novelist plays with his siblings

The other dimension of Catholicism which is so attractive to Catholics is its emphasis on community—an emphasis which is diametrically opposed to the emphasis on the individual which is so much part of American culture. Catholicism teaches and Catholics believe in their bones that we relate to God as part of a network of family, friends, and neighbors. We feel all other human behavior intuitively involves us as members of groups. Why should religion be any different? Why should we, when it comes to religion, go off into the desert by ourselves? Why desert our lovers, our neighbors, our friends, when it comes to God?

So we express our intense communal relations at every level of our lives and most particularly in the neighborhood parish which *is* the church for us. Catholics cluster, they bond, they converge, they swarm. Catholicism in James Joyce's happy phrase means "Here comes everybody!" We draw our boundaries out as wide as we can and, in our better moments, include within the boundaries even those who think they are outside. It's hard to stop being a Catholic. Those rigid people who try to draw the boundaries tightly (so as to exclude the ones with whom they disagree) misunderstand what Catholicism is about. We are not a religion for only the saved, much less for those who think that they are saved. We are a religion for everyone. Even those who have been excommunicated are still Catholics. The only way one can get out is by formally and explicitly announcing that they have renounced the faith or by joining another denomination. Even then neither the church nor your own imagination gives up on you. Never!

It's more fun being Catholic because it's more fun to belong to something than to be a religious lone wolf. Do I have evidence for my claim that Catholics are (on the average) more communal than others? Does one really need evidence? I wonder. However, in a multination study of family life, my colleagues in the International Social Survey Program discovered that in virtually every country Catholics are more likely to live with their parents or to live close to them, to visit them often, and to talk to them often on the phone. The same things are true of relationships with children and siblings and even with other relatives. Catholics, as I say, tend to swarm.

I administer this questionnaire to my students at both the University of Arizona and the University of Chicago on the first day of my class in the sociology of religion. The young people refuse to believe that such behaviors have anything to do with religion. Then when I present the findings (the same as in the multination study), they tell me that "everyone knows Catholics are more communal!"

Yeah!

It is fun to belong to something, it is fun to believe that God is close to us, loving us like a spouse, a parent, a friend. That's why Catholics stick to their church, come what may. That's why the confusion and the chaos in the church in the years since the end of the Second Vatican Council has not driven

Andrew Greeley, 1954: a newly ordained priest ready to have fun

7

Catholics out of the church despite all the attempts of us priests and bishops to drive them out! Despite the creeps and the party-poopers, the puritans and the spoil-sports, the kill-joys and parade ruiners, Catholicism is too much fun to leave.

It always has been.

It is not likely to change.

Deo gratias!

Andrew M. Greeley, a native of Chicago, is a priest, a distinguished sociologist, and a bestselling novelist.

I like being Catholic because the faith is ancient, and ancient in my family and clan, and so connects me to men and women I love, some I have never known. Because the Story is riveting, enticing, entrancing, enormously powerful and persistent. Because of the mythic magic of the Mass. Because Catholicism is about Light. Because all of Christ's message can be boiled down to a single word: love. Because His story has an eerie human genius and truth, a mother with a child, a mysterious powerful father, the puzzled brave stepfather. Because I need to believe in a future driven by love and in a life after this life defined wholly by love. Because divinity is everywhere and in everything and Catholic saints above all others have articulated this with passion and poetry. Because more than any other faith it is about hope beyond sense; and so to me is the bravest of faiths; and so I eat it happily, carried along by its utterly human stew of foolishness and grace, cruelty and joy.

—Brian Doyle, journalist
Portland, Oregon

Chapter   Two

IT'S GOOD TO BE CATHOLIC

Ten Good Reasons to Be Catholic

BY KATHY COFFEY

Number One: We are the community that remembers Jesus.
I see this especially in the surrendered lives of those who show us Christ's
face, his hands and eyes and words and compassionate touch. We call it
the Mystical Body, but it means that we recognize Jesus in the laughter
and voices of those around us: little kids, retired folks, teenagers, all those
in whom Christ continues to take flesh.

While all Christian communities remember Jesus, Catholics do so in
a particular, liturgical way. When someone we love has died and we try to
recapture memories of that person, we usually do so through our senses.
We remember Grandma's tortillas, or the song that Grandpa sang off-key.
One of my friends whose husband died broke down when she smelled his
after-shave lingering in his shirts.

It is the same with Jesus. When we remember him, we grope for the
touch of his hands on a loaf of bread, the sound of his voice telling stories, the words he breathed into wine. We find him still in the simplest
human activities, eating and drinking, gathering with friends and telling
stories.

When I was teaching undergraduates at Regis Jesuit University in
Denver, three students asked, "Mrs. Coffey, are you coming to our Mass
for Holy Thursday?" I was slightly taken aback. It's not often that 19-year-
old boys invite me to Mass with major enthusiasm. They did not get this

excited about the English class I was teaching. So I went. And what I saw is not unique; similar liturgies occur around the country.

My college students were so dressed up I could barely recognize them. They had vested for the high holy days. They carried beautiful banners; they processed reverently with bells and baskets and bread and wine. All the while they chanted Tom Conry's song, "All people here who remember Jesus, brother and friend. All who hold to his mem'ry, all who keep faith in the end." It's for moments like those that I keep returning.

Number Two: Catholicism has universality.
We Irish have our gifts, but *mariachi* music isn't one of them. So I've been grateful to the people with Spanish and African-American backgrounds for the richness, the color, the vibrancy they bring to our faith. No one tradition has the resources to meet the challenges of the next century. Yet in the church, we find the pluralism that the human race will need to survive.

Some examples may clarify Number Two. In Santa Fe, I once attended a workshop that concluded around 10 P.M. It had been a wonderful day, but we were all tired. So when we heard that we'd end with the blessing, the Anglos assumed, with typical efficiency, "one size fits all"—one blessing for all of us. Wrong. Every single person got an individual blessing. I learned that night that there are some things so important they don't fit on a tight schedule.

What universality means in practical terms is that on Wednesday night I can visit a poor parish where the people come through pouring rain to sit on folding chairs in a gym with a leaky roof. Then on Saturday, I can fly to a megachurch which cost millions, a parish with the highest concentration of M.D.'s and Ph.D.'s in the country. In both places, we explore the same, unchanging Sunday Gospel that crosses all the differences.

Number Three: Catholics make bold claims.
Sometimes these startle people of other traditions. "Who do you think you are?" they might ask. We answer, seriously and repeatedly, we are Christ's presence on earth today. We cooperate with God to build God's

kingdom in this world. In the Eucharist, we say that through bread and wine we become the body of Christ. It may sound arrogant, but this is what Jesus meant when he said, "You will do greater things than I have done." How's that for a bold claim?

Each sacrament is similar, but take Confirmation for another example. The Spirit comes, we say, through this ritual gesture of imposing hands and this chrism signed on the forehead. The same Spirit transformed terrified disciples who'd locked themselves in a room in fear of the authorities. The same Spirit transfigured the known world through the efforts of 12 people who weren't especially bright or powerful. This same Spirit is ours.

Number Four: The church is a family.
The church is at its best when we are like family: When we lose sight of that, we become legalistic, antiseptic and cold. Sometimes it's a dysfunctional family, but it gives my children something broader and deeper than anything I could ever give them alone. My oldest son, David, recently returned from Chicago where he attended Mass at O'Hare Airport. He said something I've waited 23 years to hear: "That's what I love about being Catholic. It's the same everywhere in the world. I know what to do when they take up the collection!"

When the rite of election was celebrated at the cathedral in San Antonio, Texas, one little girl could barely reach the Book of the Elect on the altar. So the bishop held her up. She tried to copy her name off her name tag, and got the first name fine. But when the last name proved too much, the bishop wrote it for her—what any kind grandfather would do!

Number Five: We have splendid heroes and heroines.
In a presidential campaign, the Republicans associate themselves with Lincoln, and the Democrats remind us that they are the party of Kennedy. We could borrow that tactic, saying stoutly, "We are the Church of Catherine of Siena, Francis of Assisi, Ignatius Loyola, Thomas More, Teresa of Avila, Vincent de Paul, Elizabeth Ann Seton, Thomas Merton, Dorothy Day, Oscar Romero, Rigoberta Menchu, the martyrs of El Salvador . . ."—and the litany could continue.

Number Six: Catholics always have something to celebrate.
Guardian angels in October, the Communion of Saints in November, Our
Lady of Guadalupe, St. Nicholas and Santa Lucia in Advent, Catholic
Education Week in January, Mardi Gras, "burying the Alleluia" on Ash
Wednesday and resurrecting it on Easter, Pentecost and the Marian
feasts—the list seems infinite. I even heard about a Hispanic parish with
an Irish pastor, where they had a fiesta for St. Patrick's Day!

Number Seven: We draw on a rich spirituality.
I know of no other tradition that celebrates the sacredness of the ordinary
as we do. All our sacraments name and claim the divine depth that sus-
tains ordinary life. So our symbols that speak most eloquently are drawn
from the most usual, earthly things: wheat and vine, water, oil, touch.
Such a sacramental theology says that even when we are not aware of it, a
wondrous grace and mystery surround us always. Just as the bread and
wine are transformed, so are we. The words "this is my body" are not spoken only over bread, but also over us.

*Number Eight: We take staunch stands on peace and
justice.*
Each locale boasts its own examples, but across the United States homeless
shelters, hospices, soup kitchens, battered women's shelters, AIDS treat-
ment centers, literacy programs, day-care centers, hospitals and schools are
sponsored and staffed by the Catholic Church. In many parts of the country we sponsor immigration services and tutoring in English. Internation-
ally the work for justice continues through agencies like Catholic Relief
Services. When the government proposed welfare cuts that would endan-
ger the poor, the Catholic bishops protested loudly and forthrightly.

These clear actions and positions are balanced by the humility to
admit we can't do it all. As the prayer of Archbishop Oscar Romero said,
our limitations are an opportunity for the Lord's grace to enter and complete our work.

Number Nine: The church can contain tensions.
This may seem odd, but I relish an image of church like a huge tent

or umbrella under which everyone can fit. Sometimes we seem to be splitting our seams, but we all still stay because this is where we belong; this is home. It is a tension into which we can relax, a struggle that can be lived.

Somehow the Catholic Church holds it all in balance: the treasures of the Vatican art galleries and the poverty of the Franciscans; the exuberance of the charismatics and the quietness of centering prayer, drums, guitars, trombones—and Gregorian chant. Any other church would have a million splinter groups: We contain it all. As James Joyce says, the Catholic Church means "Here comes everybody!"

Number Ten: Fill in the blank.
Name your favorite reason for being Catholic.

Kathy Coffey, editor and author, is the winner of seven awards from the Catholic Press Association and a recipient of the Foley Poetry Award. She lives in Denver, Colorado, with her husband and four children.

≈✿≈

Ten Good Reasons to Raise Your Kids Catholic
BY MICHAEL LEACH

1. So they'll have some rules to reject when they're teenagers.
2. So they'll have some rules to reconsider when they have kids of their own.
3. So they'll have values to cherish for the rest of their lives.
4. So they'll have something to hang on to when times are bad.
5. So they'll have at least a raggedy Good News Bible somewhere in their house or apartment that they can read for wisdom when they're older and interested.

6. So they'll come to know that every person wears the face of Christ in a different way, even those who seem to be enemies.

7. So they'll have an experience of faith in community.

8. So they'll know that Christmas is about the gift of love in their hearts.

9. So they'll know about Jesus' death and resurrection and understand that life is more than suffering.

10. So they'll know that heaven begins on the spot where they're standing and that they are here for God and that God is with them always.

~❧~

Fifty Things Catholics Like Best About Being Catholic

COMPILED BY FATHER WILLIAM A. BURKE FROM PARISHIONERS AT OUR LADY OF LORETTO CHURCH IN HOMEWOOD, ILLINOIS

1. Midnight Mass
2. Babies at Baptism
3. The smell of burning incense
4. The travels of Pope John Paul II
5. The Sacraments, all of them
6. The joy of a wedding Mass
7. The strong feeling of belonging to a wider family.
8. Mary
9. Children's Masses
10. Organ music, especially wild solos
11. Singing together as one voice
12. Everything about Christmas
13. Advent wreaths
14. Holy Week
15. Holy Thursday Procession
16. The Stations of the Cross
17. The Veneration of the Cross
18. Good Friday
19. Easter Sunday, all of it

20. Palm Sunday
21. Palms
22. Ashes smudged on your forehead
23. The smell of candles
24. St. Blaise Blessing
25. The flickering glow of vigil lights
26. The May Crowning
27. All Saints' Day
28. Stories about saints
29. St. Francis of Assisi
30. St. Patrick
31. St. Joseph
32. The Sacred Heart
33. The Lord's Prayer
34. The Rosary
35. Church bells
36. Anointing the sick
37. Scripture
38. Good homilies
39. The Consecration at Mass
40. Holy Communion
41. The Sign of Peace
42. The red Sanctuary light
43. The golden tabernacle
44. Medals
45. Crosses
46. The Sign of the Cross
47. Scapulars
48. A child at First Communion
49. Stained glass
50. Beautiful churches

Catholicism finds God just about everywhere, around every corner, under every leaf, in the eyes of a child and the eyes of a very old person. God is like a storm at sea, and God is like a quiet, clear, star-filled night sky. Jesus Himself used the metaphor of a loving Father to help us understand God, and St. Augustine of Hippo, Blessed Julian of Norwich, and Pope John Paul I declared that God is also our Mother. Catholicism rushes to embrace the good, the true, the beautiful wherever they may be found.

—Mitch Finley, author and journalist
Spokane, Washington

The poet John Fandel once wrote that we are more likely to pray in our misery than in our joy—that an ingrown toenail makes us more aware of God than a starry night. He's so right. And maybe one reason is the church's special orientation, its reflection of life's travails and crises, and the unique lesson it imparts of the triumph that is in tragedy and seemingly utter defeat. There could have been no Resurrection without the Passion, and for me there is no easy meeting of life's trials without the church of the Cross. I can understand my problems better because of the church's history of triumph over adversity, and I can cope better with life by having the reservoirs of Catholicism to draw upon.

—John Deedy, journalist
Rockport, Massachusetts

JMJ—CATHOLICISM'S FIRST FAMILY

A long time ago in a galaxy near at hand, children in Catholic schools printed the letters JMJ on top of their papers. The letters stood for Jesus, Mary, and Joseph—the first family of their faith. Later in high school they wrote AMDG—Ad Majorem Dei Gloriam—*but there would be no glory, no greater path back Home, without those first steps to Bethlehem taken by a carpenter, his pregnant wife, and their beloved son. JMJ remains a fitting acronym for the birth of Catholic faith.*

> I like being Catholic because, in my darkest moments, I've known that Jesus came to earth so that I would have abundant life, and that is what I have.
>
> —Fran Morgan
> Deer Park, New York

> I like being a Catholic because we love Jesus' mother, who is our mother, too.
>
> —Nadine Yeldig
> Beaverton, Oregon

I was named Joseph for my father. When I looked into our family's background I discovered why. In 1929, my father was baptized in a small French Canadian Catholic Church in northern Maine. The custom in those days was to record in the parish registry, every baptized boy with the name Joseph and every baptized girl with the name Mary, in addition to their chosen Christian and family names. This meant every little boy and girl in town was named for the parents of Jesus. When I first came across this I thought it was curious custom. It was much later that the significance of this began to take meaning for me. With this simple tradition, they all became the guardians, parents, family of Jesus—ready to care for the infant Lord. It was this that made me aware of the gift of being named Joseph.

—Joseph Durepos, literary agent
Downers Grove, Illinois

❧

Jesus
BY JOSEPH GIRZONE

I like being Catholic because that's where I first learned about Jesus. Jesus is the soul of my faith. I never tire of discovering more about him and learning more from him and sharing what I have learned with others. Catholicism, at its heart, is coming to "know God and Jesus Christ whom he has sent" (John 17:3).

My religion is very simple then. It is a relationship with God, an intimacy with Jesus. Over the years people have asked me about Jesus. My *Joshua* books have given them the impression that I'm some sort of expert. But I'm not. Jesus and his message are most important to me, and I've tried my whole life to understand what Jesus was like and what he was trying to teach, but I'm no more an expert than anyone else. I've come to understand that the reason my books are popular is that they confirm what so many people already know, in their own hearts, what Jesus was like, and is still like.

If I have a facile way of putting these ideas into words, I have my Catholic faith to thank. I had an excellent theological and scriptural training. Being a monk, I was taught early on how to meditate and grow in the contemplative life. In the seminary Scripture was the bread of our meditations and the wine of our contemplation. And we were able to draw on more than 1900 years of inspired thought from the great mystical teachers of our faith.

So after all this training and so many years of trying to make Jesus real in my own heart and in the hearts of my parishioners, an image of Jesus has evolved. It is a beautiful Jesus, a living reflection of his Father, the God of love. The depth of that love is far more powerful than anything we imagined as children, or can imagine now.

It has taken me a lifetime to realize just a little of what Jesus is really like. And it's very simple. He became one of us to show us how to enjoy in a loving and wholesome way the beautiful life his Father gave us in making us human. If we feel uncomfortable seeing Jesus as human, if we insist on seeing him only as divine, we deprive ourselves of the joy and comfort he came to give us in becoming one of us.

Isn't it interesting that when Jesus first began his public life, he shocked the townsfolk because he could talk so inspiringly about God? "Where did he get this from?" they asked. "Isn't he the carpenter's son?" For the 30 years he lived in Nazareth, Jesus never came across as having the "odor of sanctity." To all appearances he was just one of the townsfolk. His exquisite holiness passed unnoticed because his life was normal and uncluttered with artificial religious practices. All that people saw was a person in love with everything alive, from his Father in heaven to a lizard scurrying in the dust. Jesus was a person uninterested in impressing anyone, a man of great integrity and compassion. To this day we do an injustice to Jesus if we push him away from us and insist that he act "properly," the way we think God should act. To know how God acts, we need to see how Jesus, in fact, acted.

Isn't it marvelous that Jesus chose a wedding party to introduce his ministry? It was a feast filled with laughter, affection, and hope. He gave the guests an extra 150 to 180 gallons of choice wine after they had finished in only three days the original 8-day supply. How comfortable this God in the flesh felt with his human companions! What a myriad of messages in this simple story!

As Jesus went from village to village he rubbed elbows with the common people. We can see him walking through the narrow streets lined with shops of every sort, with the odors of unwashed peasants haggling over the price of fish or cloth or beads. These were his people, the sheep that he understood so well and loved so tenderly, creatures that nice people shunned because they were dirty and uneducated. What a wonderful God who teaches

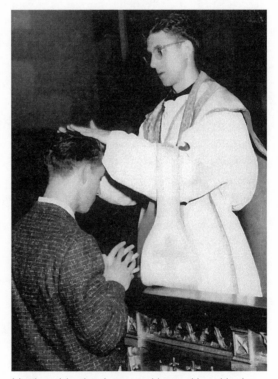

Newly ordained and eager to bless and be a blessing

us not to judge by appearances, and to see and love the good in what the world looks upon as crude and uncouth!

Now that I am older, of course, I no longer think of God as a human with a form or sex but as a being of majestic beauty and goodness wrapped in a warm and glorious light, enveloping me in a shelter of love. So to see his son walking the back streets of Jerusalem with the poor and downtrodden evokes awe and gratitude at his exquisite humility. There was no need for expressions of admiration or veneration that marked the approach of the Pharisees. Jesus' humility was his invitation to draw close to a God who cared for his children and who understood their frailty unlike any high priest on earth.

In the house of Simon, the chief Pharisee, Jesus wasn't welcomed with the ordinary marks of courtesy extended to other guests, which he neither needed nor desired. When a notorious prostitute entered the house and fell down before him and washed his feet with her tears, dried them with her hair, and anointed them with perfumed oil, she shocked the pious guests. Jesus told them that her sins were forgiven because she loves much, and hinted that she is more acceptable to God than the Pharisee who scrupulously observed all the commandments but never learned to love. "Her sins, as many as they may be, are forgiven because she loves much" (Luke 7:47). God saw in her heart a love that reached out to the troubled and the lonely and the needy among her neighbors, a love that was dry in the hearts of the righteous. "You judge by what you see on the surface; I judge by what I see in people's hearts" (John 7:24).

The story of the Samaritan woman also tells us much about Jesus and his judgment of people's private lives. After preaching a high ideal of marriage, he searches out a woman married five times and presently living with a man she never bothered to marry, and picks her to be the missionary announcing the Good News to her village. Again Jesus saw beneath the surface of a troubled and complicated life, a goodness unseen by others, a goodness that touched God's heart. How different from the way we treat such people in our churches, forbidding them to approach God because they are sinners, as if divorce and remarriage was the only sin!

I often wonder how Jesus, who chose to call sinners to himself and embrace them, looks upon us as we turn people away who come to embrace him.

One day Jesus tried to escape from a teeming crowd and flee to the other side of the lake. Approaching the shore Jesus saw the same people gathering again. They had run around the lake to be with him! "I feel so sorry for them," he told his apostles. "They are like sheep without a shepherd" (Mark 6:34). Jesus spent the rest of the day with them. He knew their sins. He wanted to be with them. He knew every detail of their lives but did not call them sinners. He called them "sheep without a shepherd." He gave a touching and unforgettable sermon, one that showed concern for their pain and troubled hearts.

"Why are you all so worried and anxious?" Jesus asked them, and us. "Look at the flock of birds over there! They do not sow, nor reap, nor gather into barns. Your heavenly Father takes care of them. You are worth more than all the flocks of birds in the world, yet all you do is worry. Stop worrying. Our heavenly Father knows your needs and takes care of you. So do not be concerned about what you wear or what you will eat. Seek to do my Father's will and all other things will be given to you besides."

The tenderness with which Jesus spoke to sinners! The assurance he offered them! He didn't approve of sin or the evil that comes to us when we sin. But he was not obsessed with sin the way so many of us are. He focused on God and the goodness in life, and made people feel comfortable with a Father who loves them and cares for them.

This is the Jesus I have come to know over the years. It is a Jesus who asks us to trust his love and open our hearts to his friendship so he can become our companion and give us strength and wisdom and comfort. And when we fail, he will pick us up and encourage us, staying with us as we continue on the way.

This is the Jesus who is the soul of our faith.

Joseph Girzone is a priest and the author of the best-selling Joshua Series, as well as *A Portrait of Jesus, Never Alone,* and *Jesus: His Life and Work.*

❧

Jesus, Model of Love

BY POPE JOHN PAUL II

*There are three things that last, faith, hope, and love; and
the greatest of these is love.*

—*I Cor. 13:13*

Jesus is the prophet of love—that love which St. Paul confesses and proclaims
in the words, so simple and at the same time so profound, in the passage from
the letter to the Corinthians. *In order to know what true love is, what its char-
acteristics and qualities are, we must look at Jesus,* at his life and his conduct.
Words will never render the reality of love so well as its living model does.
Even words, as perfect in their simplicity as those of the first letter to the
Corinthians, are only the image of this reality: the reality, that is, of which we
find the complete model in the life and behavior of Jesus Christ.

In the succession of generations, there have been and there are men
and women who have effectively imitated this perfect model. We are all
called upon to do the same. *Jesus came above all to teach us love.* It consti-
tutes the content of the greatest commandment he left to us. If we learn
to put it into practice, we will reach our purpose: eternal life.

Love, in fact, as the Apostle teaches, "does not come to an end." While
other charisms and also the essential virtues in the Christian's life end together with earthly life and pass away, love does not pass; it never ends. It
is precisely the essential foundation and content of eternal life. And therefore "the greatest of these is love."

❧

I see from the standpoint of Christian orthodoxy. For me the
meaning of life is centered in our redemption by Christ and what
I see in the world I see in its relation to that.

—Flannery O'Connor, novelist

The church is unique in that it is governed by a vision that has not changed in two thousand years. It tells us, in just about as many words, that we are not accidental biological accretions, we are creatures of a divine plan; that the God who made us undertook to demonstrate his devotion to us as individual human beings by submitting to the pain and humiliation of the cross. Nothing in that vision has ever changed, nothing at all, and this is for all Christians a mind-shaking, for some a mind-altering certitude, with which Christians live, in our earnest if pitiable efforts to clear the way for a love that cannot be requited.

—William F. Buckley, Jr., author

To me, Catholicism is all about the fact that life is very short and that we all belong to something much bigger than is immediately obvious. We are part of a 15-billion-year-old universe, and we come and go like shooting stars. But the deeper, more profound reality is that at the heart of this universe is a source that is trustworthy, loving, and generous beyond comprehension. This is our source and our destiny, and it's revealed to us through Jesus Christ in the way he lived his life.

—Robert Ludwig, director of university
ministry (DePaul University)
Chicago, Illinois

༄

There's Something About Mary

BY THERESE J. BORCHARD

About ten years ago, when I was nineteen years old, I made a pilgrimage to Lourdes, France.

I didn't have any great expectations as I was in France at the time and was simply tagging along with two friends who had their hearts set on visiting the place. I was much more excited about planning my future adventure to Lisieux, the hometown of my patron saint.

However, as our train stopped at the platform right outside the shrine at Lourdes, I could not deny that something mystical surrounded us. A scent of mystery hung in the air.

It was dusk as we climbed the long walkway to the majestic basilica with its steeples piercing the clouds, drawing back the last shards of sunlight like magnets. The River Gave, circling the church, led our footsteps to the magnificent grotto.

When I saw the rows of crutches hanging over the grotto like useless matchsticks, and the countless votive candles burning incessantly inside the cave, I understood why my mother, grandmother, and several friends had special devotions to Mary. I had been like doubting Thomas in the Gospel of John, who needed to touch Jesus and place a hand in his side before believing that the Son of God had indeed risen from the dead and appeared to the others. I knew at that moment there was something about Mary.

Two years later I found myself at the shrine of Our Lady of Guadalupe in Mexico, again without any intention of making a pilgrimage. I was en route to Acapulco with three friends on our spring break from college. Two of my friends were Cuban American, the other Mexican, and they all had a strong urge to pray at the famous site in Mexico City.

Like the moment I had stepped off the train at Lourdes, the miracles of Guadalupe overwhelmed my senses. Hundreds of people were making the Stations of the Cross on their knees, despite concrete rough enough to shred cheese. Those inside the church offered prayers of intercession to Mary and lit votive candles as visible signs of their sincerity. I looked at the original cloak made of Castilian roses that Mary had presented to the humble Juan Diego atop Tepeyac Hill in December of 1531, and again I knew: the faith of Catholics in the mother of Jesus was as rich and real as the roses themselves.

Those two trips changed the way I saw Our Lady. Before witnessing her power at Lourdes and Guadalupe, I believed that if I went directly to God, to Jesus Christ himself, there was no need in wasting time with his mother. I mean, isn't it faster to go the direct route?

My two pilgrimages taught me that Mary has a maternal responsibility to all of her children on earth. And she takes that responsibility to heart. How consoling that is.

Not only does Mary hear our prayers and intercede for us on behalf of her son, she teaches us about God.

Who could be more qualified?

She carried the Light of the World within her womb; she nursed the boy who would later change water into wine; she instructed the Greatest Teacher in the ways of faith; she raised the Son of Man who rose from the dead and is risen today. Who could know him better?

I can write and speak and explain how God becomes man in the person of Jesus Christ until I have no more words to use, but it makes no sense to me without mention of his mother. The fact that Jesus was born of a woman, just like you and me, makes Incarnation possible, and makes Christianity real.

Is it any wonder that the richest cathedrals in the world, the most famous paintings, the most beautiful music, and the most precious literature have been erected, painted, composed, and written in devotion to Mary, the mother of Jesus? She teaches us about God. She brings us hope. She embodies love.

The most lasting lesson from my pilgrimages was this: Mary never goes away. She transcends time, speaks all languages, and knows all cultures. She continues to appear to the most vulnerable among us, in the most fragile, war-stricken places of earth to speak her message of enduring peace.

And she is persistent. How else could she have made a believer of me?

❧

I found God when I was pregnant at thirty years old. The funny thing was I had been working for a Catholic organization for almost ten years. I guess you could say I had a 9 to 5 relationship with God. I never prayed. I didn't have to, my life was good.

Pregnancy was tough for me. I was so afraid of everything. I worried obsessively and I cried a lot. I was surrounded by lots of friends and family, but I never felt so alone in my life. I began praying.

When I went into labor I called on Mary for the first time. I said only four words: "Don't abandon me now." From that moment on I have felt a gentle calming presence around me. I had a truly wonderful birthing experience and when I met my son, Sam, for the first time I felt a love unlike any other.

When we came home from the hospital there awaited a gift from a lovely person in my life, Sister Mary Madden. The gift was a picture of Mary holding her infant Jesus above a prayer that begins:

Remember O most gracious Virgin Mary, that never was it known that anyone who fled to your protection, implored your help or sought your intercession was left unaided . . .

My son led me to God. I am now learning the catechism and can honestly say I like becoming a Catholic. The greatest gift I can give my son is the knowledge of this beautiful tradition.

I have been very fortunate to experience the mysteries of God's grace. I now pray every day, but my prayers are much different from when I began praying. I now know that my life is truly good and I look forward to the day when I can say, "I like *being* Catholic."

—Patti Byrns, sales consultant
Tarrytown, New York

In those days [at St. John's boarding school in Beaumont, England] I remember a special reverence for Our Lady, to whom I appealed as a mother herself. I hadn't the capacity (even now I am not comfortable with the abstraction) to imagine infinity. I accepted it as a gospel truth that the Mother of God was "infinitely" wonderful, which meant to me that she was many times as wonderful as my own mother, but this hypothesis I had difficulty with: How was it possible to be many times more wonderful than my mother? I never asked any of the priests for help with that one. After all, I reasoned, they did not know Mother, so they might find the question surprising, impudent even. I knew that would not be the case if they had *known* Mother. But Our Lady became in my mind an indispensable character of the heavenly cloister.

—William F. Buckley, Jr., author

※

Go to Joseph

BY JOSEPH M. CHAMPLIN

About fifteen years ago, while preparing to write a book on healing in the Catholic Church, I took the train to nearby Montreal. My purpose was to ask for God's blessing on this project at St. Joseph's Oratory, a famous shrine made possible by the prayers and miraculous cures of Brother André.

Brother André was Alfred Besette, a frail but unusually devout young man who sought at 25 to enter the Congregation of Holy Cross in Montreal as a religious brother. Even though his pastor told that community's leaders, "I am sending you a saint," they hesitated to accept Besette because of his poor health. (Their fears proved unfounded. He died in 1937 at 91.)

Soon after Alfred began his life as Brother André, he manifested a unique ability to heal the spiritually and physically sick. And he did so always by calling upon the help of St. Joseph, the husband of Mary and protector of Jesus. His lifelong dream and endeavor was to build a huge church dedicated to Joseph.

A large statue on the grounds today greets visitors and illustrates the spirituality of Blessed André Besette. This sculptured image portrays St.

Joseph with the Christ child in his arms
and includes the Latin motto *Ite ad Joseph*
("Go to Joseph"), chiseled into its base.

A corridor of candles within the
church reflects the results of prayers seeking St. Joseph's help. Suspended from the
ceiling are a vast array of crutches, canes
and braces, even a pair of children's shoes.
Those discarded items give silent witness
to healings attributed to the prayer of
Blessed Brother André and to the many
pleas seeking the assistance of St. Joseph.

Catholics believe that Jesus, his mother,
and all the saints in heaven, help all of us
still here on earth. Next to Jesus and Mary,
believers probably call upon Joseph more
often for aid than upon any other saint.

The Catholic Church has also officially invoked St. Joseph's assistance
in contemporary times. In 1870, during a difficult period of the church's
history, Pope Paul IX declared Joseph to be the "Patron of the Catholic
Church."

In 1962, Pope John XXIII, who had a great devotion to Saint Joseph,
directed that his name be inserted in the first eucharistic prayer, placing it
after the name of Mary and before the apostles, popes, and martyrs.

In 1989, Pope John Paul II published an apostolic exhortation, "On
the Person and Mission of Saint Joseph in the Life of Christ and of the
Church."

Joseph is not only our helper. Like all the saints, he is also a model. Three
aspects of his life are especially meaningful for me since I bear his name.

He swiftly obeyed God's often confusing and challenging directions.
His reaction to those surely disturbing divine impulses was always the
same—immediate and unquestioning.

Told in a dream about Mary's pregnancy, when Joseph finally awoke he "did as the angel of the Lord had directed him and received her into his home as his wife" (Matthew 1:24).

Told again in a dream to flee from Herod, "Joseph got up and took the child and his mother, and left that night for Egypt" (Matthew 2:14).

Told once more in a dream to journey back home, Joseph "got up, took the child and his mother, and returned to the land of Israel" (Matthew 2:21).

He balanced hard work and constant prayer.

"Isn't this the carpenter's son?" (Matthew 13:55). "Is this not Jesus, the son of Joseph?" (John 6:42).

The church sees in Joseph a model for every worker and a support for the dignity of all work, including physical labor. Catholics have a feast of St. Joseph the Worker, established in 1955, and texts from their official prayer book on that day announce: "St. Joseph faithfully practiced the carpenters' trade. He is a shining example for all workers."

Nevertheless, as a faithful Jewish man, Joseph would have also regularly attended the synagogue on the Sabbath, recited the prescribed meal prayers and sung the psalms. In addition, he probably sought to pronounce over 100 times daily the *berakah* or blessing formula, acknowledging with praise and gratitude those large and small gifts received from God throughout the day.

He presumably died in the arms of Jesus and Mary.

Joseph disappears from the gospels after the finding of Jesus in the temple at age 12. We only know that Christ went down with his mother and father and "was obedient to them" (Luke 2:51).

It does not seem unreasonable to assume that he died at home and in their arms. St. Joseph thus has become, among other titles, "Patron of the Dying."

Even for those of us who slip into sleep seemingly seconds after our head hits the pillow, there are a few moments of consciousness before that deeper slumber arrives.

I learned a long time ago to recite over and over in my mind a few prayerful phrases while waiting for sleep to come.

"Dear Mother in heaven, I offer to you the rest I am about to take. Sleep should also remind me of death. Jesus, Mary, and Joseph be with me at that last hour."

I've been a priest for more than forty years, and I still say that prayer each night.

Joseph M. Champlin is rector of the Cathedral of the Immaculate Conception, Syracuse, New York, and the author of more than thirty books on Catholicism with more than 10 million copies in print.

❧

My great aunt was once befriended—perhaps even saved—by a saint. When her husband of sixteen years died suddenly from a heart attack at the age of forty-two, Rose St. Louis found herself with four children to rear and a tangle of messy financial matters. Yet instead of doubting her faith, instead of becoming bitter with God for taking away her cherished husband so soon, she turned to Him for courage and guidance.

Like so many other Christians in the history of the Roman Catholic Church, she chose to find her way to God through the aid of a saint.

"Saint Joseph was the head of God's family and I had just lost the head of mine, so it seemed appropriate that I turn to him," she told me. "I think that going through life without a spouse and raising four children is incredibly difficult, and Saint Joseph helped me tremendously in making the right decisions and in guiding me through the day-to-day issues so that I could raise my children properly."

She told me that without Saint Joseph's supportive presence, she might never have made it. Today, she still prays to Saint Joseph when she needs a warm and compassionate listener. He has become her trusted friend and spiritual guide.

—Anne Gordon, journalist
Cleveland, Ohio

INTERLUDE

Cokie Roberts, who likes being Catholic, loves her husband, Sam Roberts, who likes being Jewish. Together they love their children with all their hearts. Cokie and Sam are one of a million interfaith couples in the United States who are building new bridges between love and faith. Being an interfaith family is both a challenge and an opportunity. Here is an excerpt from a letter that Cokie wrote to her children:

Lee and Becca, I have no fear for you. You might not easily be able to define yourselves as Catholic, or Jewish, or both. But you are knowledgeable about and interested in both traditions, and we have confidence you will carry them on. Daddy and I have watched Becca care for my sister as she was dying, Lee rise early in the morning to drive for soup kitchens. We've rejoiced in the way you readily assume responsibility for yourselves and others, the way you defend your beliefs, the way you live your lives. We have seen you pray at Holy Days and at Sunday Mass, light candles on the Hanukkah menorah and on the Advent wreath. Dear children, we can call your name. You are people of principle.

With love and admiration,

Mamma

FROM MATH TO MYSTERY

There isn't any question that my view of the world, my view of
life, my view of myself, my view of family, my view of work in the
world was deeply informed by my faith, which is Catholic.

—William J. Bennett, educator
and author

Catholic education still keeps the light burning.

—Charles Osgood, news correspondent

The whole conversation today about values in education emulates
what's been happening in Catholic schools. The rest of the country's coming around to what Catholic educators have always
done.

—Cokie Roberts, television journalist

The Value of Catholic Education

BY BRET D. THOMAS

Most of what I treasure about the Catholic tradition traces back to my
years of Catholic schooling. For sixteen memorable years, talented laymen
and women, sisters of Notre Dame de Namur, and brothers and priests of
the Society of Mary (Marianists) shared with me not only what they knew
of literature, grammar, mathematics, science, music, art, and history, but

they shared with me a bit of themselves and what they knew of the church and the kingdom of God.

I was an above-average student, but not by much! A's and B's were the usual fare, but in elementary school scarlet monsters regularly stained my otherwise golden report card. Quarter after quarter, year after year, a thick red checkmark etched on the back of the card noted one glaring flaw: *does not respect the rights of others.*

My penmanship was the envy of many, and my science fair projects won many a blue ribbon. I could even recite backward the corporal works of mercy, so "What's the big deal?" I thought.

Sure I enjoyed being the center of attention and at the heart of a good laugh. And yes, I was a little disruptive, and more than just a little loud. The sisters often scolded me for not using my "indoor voice" (and my colleagues today continue their plea!). Only after years of loving discipline and compassionate challenges did I begin to understand the lesson. I was being taught that there is much more to Catholic education than recitation, memorization, reading, writing, and grades. There is the Gospel and the call to serve, love, and build community. There is the call to respect others. That precious lesson, and so many more like it, continues to influence my life as a husband, son, brother, and co-worker.

I was so taken by the mission and vision of Catholic education that following my college graduation, I packed up everything I owned in a few cardboard boxes and headed East to begin my teaching career in the Diocese of Pittsburgh. For nearly six years I taught biology in three Catholic high schools. With each lesson and lab, I was given the precious charge to not just present the ever-exciting life cycle of an earthworm or the chemical process of photosynthesis, but to point to and speak of the power and mystery of the Creator. As a teacher in a Catholic school, I had the awesome opportunity to demonstrate the values that as a student had been demonstrated to me—charity, hope, faith, love, and respect.

Even though I'm no longer in the classroom, my work as a publishing professional is influenced daily by the Catholic values that were taught to me years ago. I am constantly challenged to do my work with integrity, to grow our business successfully, and to treat my colleagues and clients re-

FACTS ABOUT CATHOLIC SCHOOLS IN THE UNITED STATES

- Catholic schools comprise the largest private school system in the world.
- Four of the top ten largest school districts in the nation are Catholic: Archdiocese of Los Angeles (327,088), Archdiocese of Chicago (239,925), Archdiocese of New York (221,105), and Archdiocese of Boston (208,739).
- More than 2,725,000 students attend Catholic schools.
- More than 650,000 teachers work in 9,650 U.S. Catholic educational institutions.
- In the country's fifty largest school districts, almost one out of every four students is involved in Catholic education.
- Most Catholic school students are Catholic. However, non-Catholic student enrollment has risen from 2.7 percent in 1970 to 13.6 percent today.
- Of all Catholic schools, 41 percent have a waiting list for admission.

spectfully. The skills and values needed to accomplish these things were nurtured in Catholic classrooms.

I am one among millions of children who have benefited from Catholic schools, being offered a high quality of education within the context of a faith-filled and prayerful community. I am not only deeply grateful, but also keenly aware of the providence of God that has led a grade school student often chastised for the volume of his voice to a magazine that is known as "the voice of Catholic education."

Bret D. Thomas is publishing director of *Today's Catholic Teacher*, Dayton, Ohio.

The Mystery of Catholicism

BY JOAN WESTER ANDERSON

Catholics love a good mystery. In fact, one of the things that characterizes Catholicism throughout history is its awareness of a world that "eye has not seen, nor ear heard."

As a child I experienced mysticism as anything which touched my core, brought forth a sense of awe, a prick of tears, an understanding that there is more to reality than meets the eye. Sometimes all it took was a whiff of incense or a snippet of chant to sense the sacred. But I also remember feeling safe because I had a guardian angel, staring at a statue that seemed to weep, and making sacrifices to alleviate someone's pain or sin. Once I asked St. Therese for a rose if the sacrifice was accepted, and you can imagine how I felt when I found a rose lying in the snow on my way home from school the next day. These were groundwork moments on which any child could build a lifelong longing for the Lord.

Things changed during the cultural sea change of the 1960s and 1970s. I cooperated with, and even learned to like, most of the church's exterior alterations. Enrolling in a charismatic prayer group, volunteering for parish ministries, and taking Bible study enriched me too. Perhaps the love of mystery I had as a child, I mused, was just a stage. Now that I was a woman, it was time to put childish things away. But then, in 1991, I wrote a book called *Where Angels Walk*, and time touched eternity once again.

The book was meant to be my last. Having raised five children while writing magazine articles (and the occasional book that nobody seemed to buy), I was eager for a career where I could wear something other than a sweatshirt with spit-up stains on the shoulder, and receive a salary, however modest, on a regular basis.

Where Angels Walk comprised true stories I'd collected from more than sixty people, including one of our sons, about moments in their lives when an angel might have intervened to bring comfort or aid. The one agent I contacted turned down the proposal on the grounds that it would "never fly." When I told friends that I was writing about heavenly messengers, they looked at me with pity and suggested I take a walk to clear my head. Clearly my less than illustrious writing career would end with a whimper, not a bang. But the echo of those long ago whispers in my spirit, the lumps in my throat, the sensing of a kingdom as close as an embrace, kept pushing me on. We all needed to remember that there was still more than met the eye.

Where Angels Walk not only found a publisher, it became a bestseller and stayed on the *New York Times* list for over a year, sell-ing more than a million copies. It also ushered in a virtual avalanche of an-gels—almost 300 books on the subject, some 200 specialty stores, an Angels Book Club, television documentaries, and numerous confer-ences.

I retrieved my soup-stained sweatshirt and returned to the keyboard to write more about things unseen. Invitations poured in from Catholic and non-Catholic groups alike to speak about these mystical spirits. People soul-starved for stories of wonder jammed auditoriums and church basements to hear about the miraculous, to experience the sacred, to plunge into mystery.

It was then that I rediscovered how much I love being Catholic. Most of the invitations had come from Protestant churches. And I, a mid-west housewife without theological training had the good fortune to speak about things in the Bible that they too had overlooked, stories of spirits who had once heralded good news and were still doing it today. I remem-ber one Presbyterian woman who, during her introduction, wistfully men-tioned the "Catholic belief in angels."

"Excuse me," I interrupted. "Angels aren't Catholic. They belong to everyone." I'll never forget the astonished look of joy on her face.

Another man wanted to know why Catholics have so many other "beings" involved in their faith. "Isn't God enough?" he asked.

"Of course," I answered. "But Catholicism is built on the concept of family. We have the Father, and Jesus his son. Mary, in a beautiful way, is everyone's Mom. Angels and saints make up the older, wiser branch of the family, similar to uncles and aunts (each with their own gifts and peculiarities) whom we often approach with requests for help or advice. And then there's us, the children of God, bumbling along, trying to make sense of it all. Isn't it great that we're not alone?"

I could almost hear centuries of propaganda falling to the ground like a thousand basketballs in that school gymnasium. Angels had become a bridge, binding all children of God together in new understanding and acceptance. Who could have imagined it?

It took Catholics a little time to hop back on the angel bandwagon because they had never been completely off it. But I still appreciate the look of wonder in the eyes of anyone born in the last 30 years or so, someone becoming aware of the miraculous part of their faith for the very first time.

But it won't be the last. Like many, I've noticed the growing popularity of things long Catholic in our new spiritual culture: monastic chants and silent retreats, pilgrims flocking to holy ground, an increase in prayer, an interest in mysticism. The mystery is back. And with it, the magic.

That's why I like being Catholic. Our faith is so vast that anything that's lost—people as well as teachings—can always be found, dusted off and brought to light, as good as new.

Joan Wester Anderson looks like an angel on her Confirmation day at St. Jerome in Chicago, Illinois

Joan Wester Anderson is the author of the best-selling *Where Angels Walk* and *The Power of Miracles.*

I remember very distinctly, one day in the middle of the afternoon, a teacher coming in and saying that they thought they had
lost an astronaut, and we were all to come into the hallway immediately. They emptied all the classrooms into this long, shot-
gun hallway, maybe a hundred yards long and all cinderblock. So
the effect was that of a sewer suddenly infested with penguins, by
which I mean that we were all on our knees praying—for Gus
Grissom, I think it was. It was not altogether lost on me that there
was something very concrete to the power of prayer, that more
was more.

> —Christopher Buckley, author

Throughout my public life . . . there is no question that the values that were built into me by both my parents as well as my education, particularly in Catholic schools, have played a major role
in . . . forming my approach to the issues and my philosophy of
what this country is all about.

> —Leon Panetta, former White House
> chief of staff

I think we are taught there is a reason for everything. I think we
are taught to accept the inevitable when it happens. I think we are
taught a sense of joy . . . A lot of that comes from Catholic education. And, of course, the Catholic home.

> —Mary Higgins Clark, novelist

INTERLUDE

The Average Catholic
BY MICHAEL LEACH

Forget the statistics. Never mind what you read in the papers. Here's the real skinny:

The Average Catholic is young, old, middle-aged, and every color of the human rainbow. She prays the rosary or chants a mantra or doesn't use words at all. He reads the diocesan newspaper or a religious magazine or, most likely, nothing "Catholic" at all. She goes to a Bible study group at the parish or to a yoga class at the civic center or watches CNN and considers from her sofa what life is all about. He reflects on the teachings of Jesus or meditates on a spiritual book or simply remembers "the chosen part of things" learned long ago. She is interested in what she is here for and what it all means and what to snack on when *Dharma and Greg* comes on. The Average Catholic does not fit easily into a square or a circle but belongs to a big triangle that holds all shapes and sizes.

The Average Catholic is grateful that her church is a moral standard bearer. He is proud of the Pope's affirmation of life wherever he goes. She wishes more leaders, in the church and in the world, would witness to the truth that all of life is sacred: the unborn and the born, the earth and all its inhabitants. The Average Catholic has a high moral standard but is reluctant to chastise anyone, other than himself, who doesn't live up to it.

The Average Catholic values the virtues of fidelity and chastity but refuses to call anyone who falls short of her values a sinner. He learned early on never to throw stones. Besides, the only sinner she's greatly familiar with is herself. When he prays the Our Father and says, "Forgive us our trespasses as we forgive those who trespass against us," the Average Catholic thinks twice. Sometimes she wonders if she'll ever get it right. He is grateful that God is Love.

The Average Catholic is rarely interested in anyone's sexual orientation. She finds public or private talk about the sexual activities of homo-sexuals or heterosexuals tasteless, and can't understand why anyone would want to flog or flaunt, persecute or parade sexuality of any kind. In his rare moments when he is in the vicinity of "being close to God," the Average Catholic knows that sex is at best a glorious distraction, and at worst nothing but trouble. She can't stop the world from emphasizing it, but she thinks it wouldn't hurt if her church spoke less about it. The worst result: a better sense of balance.

The Average Catholic loves priests and nuns, and is not alarmed by new forms of ministry. He has lived long enough to know that things change. She knows that appearances change but "the chosen part" of priesthood—service to others for the sake of the kingdom—will never change. Nor Jesus' promise: "I will be with you always, even to the end of the world."

The next time you look at the statistics, please remember: the Average Catholic is very much like you.

Chapter Five

SACRAMENTS AND MILESTONES

I like being Catholic because it offers seven ways to be in touch, literally, with the risen Christ—seven visible signs of an invisible Reality to remind us that everything ordinary is as holy as it can be.

—Mitch Finley, author and journalist
Spokane, Washington

At all the key moments of life, birth and death, love and maturity, illness and commitment, God keeps breaking into our lives. God says: "I want to be there to baptize this new child into the life of the community; I want to be there when two people promise each other fidelity for life; I want to be there when sickness strikes; I want to be there to feed my people with word and eucharist." Life, for me, would lack all integration if God were not a part of these key experiences.

—Robert F. Morneau, Auxiliary Bishop
Green Bay, Wisconsin

Sacraments are, for me, extraordinary experiences of the ordinary.
—Rosemary Haughton,
theologian and author
Gloucester, Massachusetts

❧

A Few of My Favorite Things
BY THERESE J. BORCHARD

If you had to pick the most important aspect of being Catholic according to the 63 million Catholics in the United States, what would you guess? Here are some hints . . .

- There are seven of them; however, it is the rare Catholic who has experienced all of them.
- Most of us were too young to remember the day we experienced the first one.
- They form a framework for our lives, breaking into the key moments of our living and dying.
- They were one of the first things we learned in our catechism classes.

If you guessed the sacraments, you're right! According to a *1999 National Catholic Reporter*/Gallup poll, sacraments ranked first among the top five identifiable Catholic hallmarks—the other four being spirituality, social justice, Marian doctrine, and community.

I don't know why I find this surprising. After all, for every milestone in our lives a sacrament awaits us. Soon after birth comes Baptism. In the defining moments of our childhood come our first Reconciliation, our First Communion, and our Confirmation. As we mature into adults and make a commitment to a certain vocation, many of us celebrate the sacrament of Matrimony, others the sacrament of Holy Orders. In moments of sickness or grave illness, we receive the Anointing of the Sick.

The sacraments are given to us by God as an invitation to live life to its fullest, to plunge into the ordinary events of life, and to transform them into extraordinary moments of grace. The sacraments provide a framework for Christian living. They are our Cliffs Notes for life. But just as we need to read the whole novel to gain the most benefit from Cliffs Notes, for full appreciation of the sacraments, we need to understand them against the backdrop of God's kingdom on earth—the holy sneaking gracefully into the most intimate places of our world.

The church loosely defines sacrament as "an outward sign of an inward grace," but the word most commonly refers to the seven principal liturgical rites of the Catholic tradition. Each one has its own outward sign pointing to an inward grace.

The *sacraments of initiation*:

- *Baptism*, a purifying fountain of water that welcomes newly born Christians into a loving community;
- *Eucharist*, the fresh bread of our life, the fermented wine of our salvation;
- *Confirmation*, the chrism on our foreheads anointing us with the gift of the Holy Spirit.

The *sacraments of healing*:

- *Reconciliation*, the sign of the cross assuring us of God's unending forgiveness;
- *The Anointing of the Sick*, an embrace of hands that promises everlasting life.

The *sacraments of vocation and commitment*:

- *Holy Orders*, a robe of service signifying vows of obedience, poverty, and chastity;
- *Matrimony*, a candle uniting two souls in love and fidelity.

I have to admit that I am a little old-fashioned in my understanding of the word. Before the twelfth century—when the church determined the seven sacraments that we celebrate today—the term *sacrament* was used in much broader context, referring simply to God's manifested power and love in our world.

That is how I also understand the sacraments.

I believe that a person experiences baptism when he embraces the responsibility of living as a son or daughter of God, not for this world, but for eternity. I believe there is reconciliation when two enemies drop their resentments and forgive each other in order to work for the good of God.

I believe that eucharist happens as friends gather around a table for a warm meal together, where there is bread and wine and laughter and sharing of stories. I believe that I have just witnessed a confirmation when I hear a person speak his intention to live a better life. I believe that whenever my husband and I tell each other "I love you" that we are celebrating the sacrament of matrimony.

I believe that every person who has made a radical commitment to serve God has, in some form or another, honored the sacrament of holy orders. And I believe that as a person reconciles her past in order to find peace before passing on, she is indeed observing the anointing of the sick.

Don't get me wrong, I believe the sacraments are more than pretty Hallmark moments. I believe that they are moments imbued with the presence and mystery of God, and that they help us to realize that Christ is present among us in a very real way, filling our world with love and hope in the most unexpected places.

To experience any of the seven sacraments is to open ourselves to seeing "sacraments" in their old-fashioned, wider way.

Sacraments, like Cliffs Notes, point us to the underlying meaning that we may be missing in the novel that is our life. And a glimpse of heaven on earth isn't so bad either.

"...and I ate meat on Friday, and I didn't fast during Lent, and I went to see a 'B' movie... and I..."

≈✲≈

I like being Catholic because you are forgiven for everything. You can start all over again.
—Quentin Cupp, postal worker
Annapolis, Maryland

The Sacrament of Reconciliation brings me an almost unbelievable sense of tranquility every time I receive it. There are times that I leave the confessional and I feel like I have a whole new life in front of me. I keep trying to imagine how our world would be so much better if everyone experienced such love and forgiveness.
—Dianne M. Marcus
Massapequa, New York

Bishop Robert F. Morneau appreciates this essay written by a high school junior preparing to receive the sacrament of Confirmation:

Confirmation is important to me. It's a chance to stand up and proclaim my Catholicism. God is the reason I am alive today. I want to thank him, for I am forever indebted to him and his goodness to me. I want to be a messenger of God more than I presently am. I want everyone to know who God is, what his plan for us is, and why religion is important. I want to grow as a follower of Jesus and be guided in God's direction. I want to be the best person I can be for God—that is his plan for me. I want to make him proud of me. This is my way of saying, "Thank you, God" and "I love you with all my heart." This is what Confirmation means to me.

I walked down the aisle of the church with all the other kids. My father, at the edge of a pew near the back, reached out and squeezed my arm. He had tears in his eyes. I knew then that this was an important day. At the great moment I was careful not to bite the bread. I closed my eyes and talked to Jesus. I was too

awed to hear him talk to me. Later people gave me cards and money and treated me like a man. I knew I wasn't, but I knew it was an important day—the day of my First Communion.

—Michael Leach

Receiving Communion, receiving Christ, is not a reward for being good, it is a remedy to help us remain good and become stronger in the faith. I need that.

—Father Henry Fehren
New York, New York

Last summer, at 77 years old, I was hospitalized with coronary artery disease. The doctors wanted me to have bypass surgery, but I was afraid of the risks.

When the pastor emeritus of my parish came to visit me, I felt comforted seeing the friendly face I had known for almost 30 years. He heard my confession and anointed me and gave me Holy Communion. I was so sick I don't think I was totally aware I was receiving the Sacrament of the Sick. But I felt peace, and within a few days I got the courage to go for the triple bypass surgery that saved my life.

—Agnes Gaughan,
grandmother
Bronx, New York

The sacraments keep me whole.

My core, the heart of me, is my Baptism, my Christ-ening. Since that day over fifty years ago, held over the font by my Aunt

Kay, I began a communion with other Christians, even closer than the communion I had had with my mother just two weeks before, nestled in her womb.

Marriage is the sacrament of my daily round. Over thirty years ago my wife and I pledged ourselves publicly to live a sacrament of deepening our baptismal communion with one another, to manifest to the world the communion between Christ and the Church. Through years of parenting pressures, career challenges, personal crises, in good times and in bad, in sickness and in health, our communion has held.

The Eucharist, Holy Communion, is the balm which heals all my dishonored communions.

—Walt Chura, teacher and
retreat director
Albany, New York

I like being Catholic because of the Eucharist. Through this sacrament I am given the opportunity to share communion with God.

—Robert E. Murphy,
twenty-four years old, physical therapist
Laurel, Mississippi

Justine Povlin, like millions of young girls, shines on the day of her First Communion

Being a convert, I have a greater appreciation of the sacramental life of Catholics, something born-Catholics may take for granted. My Baptism, Confirmation, and First Communion at the Easter Vigil changed my life forever.

—Jeffrey Shawhan, electrician
Dayton, Ohio

I like being Catholic and I like being married because they both
give me strength and joy.

—Vickie Leach, assistant principal
Riverside, Connecticut

I've never had an event in which the real so closely approximated
the ideal as my First Communion. I prepared for it well and thoroughly and I felt absolutely pure. I remember that feeling of purity—it was an occasion and an event that was exactly what I had

dreamed of. I was all white and everybody was all white and people were singing "Little White Guest," and it really was to me in all my life the hallmark and paradigm of purity.

And confession, too. After you had made a good and, sometimes, a difficult confession, walking out of that church and feeling a lightness and singleness was beautiful and very valuable, and I don't think the secular world has any replacements for it including the esthetic experience, which is the thing that comes closest to it. I don't think that sense of utter purity and lightness and singleness can be duplicated outside of the Church context.

—Mary Gordon, novelist

My sister Peggy and I chose to become a nun and a priest. We were the youngest two of four kids, two girls and two boys. My brother and sister married and had eleven kids. Our life choices have brought much life to all four of us—as well as to our parents and all the other people in our lives.

—Andy Costello, CSSR
Lima, Ohio

"It's his First Communion picture!
Won't he at least take off his 'shades' for that?"

When I made my First Communion I was six and it seemed as natural to me and about as startling as brushing my teeth.

—Flannery O'Connor, novelist

What I remember mostly about first holy communion was the whiteness of the costumes and my special satisfaction in finally being allowed to wear long pants, for it would be many years before I was again allowed to wear long pants. There was a sense of something important going on. The movie cameras were out, the girls in their white dresses, the gold medallion with your name engraved on it. It was life's first ritual. There would be many rituals to follow, but that inflected all rituals with, I suppose, a subconscious religious content.

—Christopher Buckley, author

I find in the sacraments of the Catholic Church the way in which God, through the persons of the Trinity and especially through Jesus Christ, is present today, equally to all. The Mass, in particular, is the place where I believe that presence is most realized. It has always been a marvel to me that the Mass knows no bounds of time or space, or race or class.

I marvel at a God who becomes one with us. I marvel even more at a God who remains with us in those human and material instruments we call sacraments. They are enough to keep anyone Catholic and to help one make the sacrifice of getting up and going to Mass.

—Rembert G. Weakland, O.S.B.,
Archbishop
Milwaukee, Wisconsin

In the end, it's the sacraments that help Catholics discover their identity.

—Richard Rohr, O.F.M.,
author and retreat master
Albuquerque, New Mexico

INTERLUDE

As I child, I was obsessive about religion. I wanted to get leprosy and be miraculously cured. I used to sleep with a little plastic cross. One morning I woke up with an imprint on my chest and I knew I had the stigmata. I ran to my mother and said, "Mom, I've got it—the stigmata!" She said, "You fool—you've slept on your crucifix."

—Mary Gordon, novelist

What I like about the Catholics is that they have this sort of mussed-up human way. You go to church, there are people of all different colors and ages, and babies squalling. You're taking a stand with these people. You're saying: "Here I am. One of the people who love God."

—Annie Dillard, author

I am a devout Catholic. It's that simple . . . It's almost quaint to use words like that, but I am.

—Mary Higgins Clark, novelist

Becoming a Roman Catholic was one of the better decisions of my life. It permitted me to love and be loved. Never having had a father, it was great to discover I had the greatest of them all . . . I am glad that I became a Catholic because it is as though I had been adopted by a noble family.

—Clare Boothe Luce

I write the way I do because . . . I am a Catholic.

—Flannery O'Connor, novelist

Chapter Six

MASS APPEAL

I derive my strength from Mass.
—Vince Lombardi

I always found comfort and joy in religion. No matter where I am, come Sunday I'll find the Catholic church. It's always been the very heart of my existence . . . perhaps the basis of it.
—Mary Higgins Clark, novelist

Attending Mass each Sunday is an anchor in my life. It's one of the things I need to do to see the power of God in my life.

—Eric Lutes, actor

I go to church every Sunday because I want to, because I have made a choice to live this way. And I believe that if I want faith, I have to go after it and pray for it and work at it.

—Maria Shriver, television journalist

Whenever you go to Mass, you run the risk of falling into grace.

—Richard J. Sklba, Auxiliary Bishop
Milwaukee, Wisconsin

❧

My Heart Got Stuck in the Daily Mass
BY PATRICIA CAROL

I am 45 years old, have worked for 22 years as a director of religious education, minister, and leader in the Unitarian Universalist Association, and now I am about to join the Roman Catholic Church. "No thinking person would do that," I am told. No thinking woman would do that. But here I am—an educated, powerful woman who can do no other. Why?

My heart got stuck in the daily Mass, and I cannot leave. Some 15 months ago, I came through the doors of the Catholic Church in spiritual crisis. In the grief of a lost marriage, I couldn't find God.

I felt the need to be with people praying but didn't want to have to explain myself or my inevitable tears, so I went to a daily Mass. I didn't know the first thing about a Mass. But that first day I knew I needed to learn the words, the prayers, the saints. I knew I had to see Advent, Lent, Christmas, and Easter. I felt the need to see the year's cycle unfold. I feel that I am hearing the stories of Jesus as if for the first time, though I've heard them my whole life.

Why do I want to join this church? Because I have felt more prayed for than at any time in my life. The prayers are for the injured, the depressed, those with back pain, those addicted—not me, and yet definitely me. Me as connected to everyone.

Why do I want to join this church? Because the saints and the examples of faithfulness are so real and compelling that they remind me to be faithful. I find myself wondering,

Father John J. Piderit, S.J., president of Loyola University College in Chicago, Illinois, says Mass for the students

"Who wrote that call to worship? Who combined these words so gently and beautifully? Who wrote that song? Who put these readings together for this day, just when I need them?"

Why do I want to join this church? Because the people come every day. Young and old, with babies and walkers, with business suits and rumpled T-shirts. They sing and say together, "Lord, hear our prayer," and move with focus to the Eucharist. I stay in my pew and feel the currents of the air around me, created by the movement of their bodies, perhaps the movement of the spirit.

Why do I want to join this church? Because I cannot pretend this did not happen and walk away.

Patricia Carol works as a conflict interventionist for churches and synagogues.

❧

Years ago, I can remember towing a car up and down the highway and finding a church to go to Mass on Sunday in all kinds of out-of-the-way places.

Early one Sunday morning I went to Mass at St. Peter's Church in downtown Charlotte. The priest, Father Sebastian, came out and asked if anybody could serve Mass.

I looked around the church. There were only five people in the whole church. The priest looked straight at me and said, "Will somebody serve Mass for me?"

I said, "Father, I'm not an altar boy, but I'll sure do whatever I can."

I did what he told me to do and served Mass. I left there and came out here (to the speedway) and won the World 600 for the first time. I always felt good about that.

—Bobby Allison, stock-car racer

There is some basic coherence to the whole phenomenon we call the Catholic Church, and we can find it by simply observing a Sunday liturgy anywhere in the world.

—Lawrence S. Cunningham,
    professor of theology (Notre Dame)
    Notre Dame, Indiana

I find it extremely comforting to know that wherever I go I can attend Mass and hear the same readings and share Holy Communion with all the Catholics of the world.

—Jeffrey Shawhan, electrician
    Dayton, Ohio

I like being a lector because I love to read the words each time as if for the very first time. I am hearer as well as speaker. I never fail to be moved or inspired by the selection—I am always, somehow, surprised!

—Lynn Schmitt Quinn, book editor
    New York, New York

I was an altar boy, but I was drummed out because I used to arrive late for seven o'clock Mass. My specialist altar boy training was for the Mass for the dead on Saturdays, the ten-thirty funerals. I was very good at that for some reason. They would always give me that, I don't know why—the priest wanted me to do it, so I did. I became very enamored of one particular young priest who was a breath of fresh air. I was eleven or twelve, and I really wanted to be like him, so I patterned my whole life after him.

—Martin Scorsese, film director

I like being an altar server because it's fun and it's nice to serve God.

—Jane Hedrick, age eleven
Old Greenwich, Connecticut

The Mass and Eucharist bring me the most joy. I've attended Mass in many locales, from the remembered pews of my youth to the air-conditioned intimacy of my parish. I've attended Mass said on the hood of a jeep in the Ardennes, a bark-covered altar in the Philippine mountains, and in the early-morning quiet of an Irish chapel. Every time I think how grateful I am to be there.

—Robert T. Reilly
Omaha, Nebraska

The most central of all of the sacraments is the Eucharist. As a priest for over fifty-four years, I have had the great joy of offering Mass almost every day of my priestly life.

It is important to remember that we offer Mass not just for ourselves and our families and friends but for the whole world each day. Quote the words in the Mass itself. We pray, "for the peace and salvation of all of the world." What a wonderful privilege this is for Catholics everywhere and for people everywhere who wish to join us in this most perfect of all prayers.

—Theodore M. Hesburgh, C.S.C.
Notre Dame, Indiana

Quite often, nothing much happens to me when I go to church. But when I get into it and listen, when I participate and am aware of the people around me and what we're there for, the Mass is pretty powerful. I reconnect with my values. The parish becomes not a random group of people but a family.

—Bernie Martin, attorney
La Grange, Illinois

There are times when being at Mass is anything but exciting. The music is banal, the sermons are trite. The people in the pews around me are irritating, and I couldn't utter a decent prayer to save my life. And then, there are times when it's the perfect place for me to be. The music is uplifting, I hear just what I need to hear. I feel a sense of oneness with my fellow parishioners and in communion with my God. And sometimes both of these sets of feelings occur at the same Mass!

Why do I go to Mass? At Mass I get fed. I know I am weak. I want to be more selfless, more charitable, more kind. I want to be braver when I hear a racist remark, stronger when my children need a firm response, purer of heart when tempted to take an easier, softer way. I want to absorb the patterns of the life of Jesus. The Host on the tongue gives strength to run the race. The wine gives heart and willingness to continue.

—Tom McGrath,
editor of *U.S. Catholic* magazine
Chicago, Illinois

Even as a Protestant, I had always wanted to kiss the feet of Jesus on the cross in a gesture of love and adoration. It was with a tremendous sense of homecoming that I experienced the Veneration of the Cross on Good Friday as part of a standard Roman Catholic liturgy.

Liturgy is the main reason I became a Catholic. God comes to us in external signs, which take our human bodies, and therefore the Incarnation, seriously: bread that must be chewed, wine that tingles the throat, incense that lingers long after Benediction.

As a convert, I found that liturgy was a vehicle that carried me to a point of communion every time, whether I felt spiritual or not.

We need ritual; humans naturally develop liturgies simply in living their lives. As surely as we have a sense of time, we have a sense of marking and regulating that time. Catholics do it in a spirit of hope and joyous anticipation; for when the Lord comes and his final glory has been revealed, we will be forever beyond time, in an eternity with him who is eternal. Until then, we are a people patiently waiting: Come, let us adore!

       —Sister Sheryl Chen, OCSO
       Dubuque, Iowa

INTERLUDE

I like being Catholic because, like a batting average, it sets a standard by which I can measure myself.

—Babe Ruth

I've got a great deal of faith in God, a great deal of dependency on God. I don't think I'd do anything without that dependency.

—Vince Lombardi

About five-thirty in the morning, while pacing the lobby, I unexpectedly ran into two of my players hurrying out. I asked where they were going at that hour—although I had a good idea. Within the next few minutes, a dozen more hurried out and I suddenly decided to go with them. They didn't realize it, but these youngsters were making a powerful impression on me with their devotion, and when I saw all of them walking up to the Communion rail, and realized the hours of sleep they'd sacrificed, I understood for the first time what a powerful ally their religion was to them in their work on the football field.

—Knute Rockne

I have always liked being Catholic because it has always seemed to me more spiritual than other ways to worship. Seeing my mother attend Mass three or four times a week, I figured it was the best way for me to show my love for God. The love and devotion of the priest and nuns also has been an inspiration to me. I know they all pray for me and my family.

—Yogi Berra

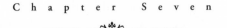

FAVORITE PRAYERS, TRADITIONS, AND RITUALS

I understand prayer not as just an act of devotion, but also as the technique of a secret alchemy for obtaining wonders, miracles and magic.

—Federico Fellini, film director

Simple gestures. Simple words. But they tell us who we are. We have a tendency to forget. And so we do it all over again—to remember.

—Richard T. Szafranski
Vassar, Michigan

My favorite prayer, which is the most powerful prayer I know, is
"Jesus, mercy."

—Martin Sheen, actor

The best prayer in the world is "Let thy will be done," because
God knows what you want. So say, "Don't give me what I want;
give me what I *need*."

—Aaron Neville, singer

༺⚜༻

The Varieties of Catholic Prayer
BY MICHAEL LEACH AND THERESE J. BORCHARD

A Sioux woman fingers the beads of her rosary at the back of a church in
South Dakota.

A Wall Street banker sits on a bench in Battery Park, watching the parade of people, and contemplating the Christ who lives in each and all of
them.

Fifteen Trappist monks chant as one in a chapel in Kentucky while
outside the roosters still sleep.

A single mother in Chicago nurses her baby and asks God to help her
forgive the man who abandoned them.

A teenager in Sacramento puts down his homework to realize again
the love he has for his grandmother, who died of Alzheimer's disease.

A priest in Puerto Rico holds out a wafer and whispers, *"Maria, el
Cuerpo de Cristo."* His parishioner says "Amen," and receives the bread of
life on the pillow of her tongue.

A mother in Colorado Springs cooks dinner for her family of five,
thinks of St. Thérèse's saying that "God is found among the pots and
pans," and offers her work to God for those who are lonely.

Ten million people from every part of the earth, all at the same time,
say "Thank you, God!" without hearing the harmony with their brothers
and sisters, but knowing the joy that comes from the prayer of gratitude.

Twenty million people tell God they're sorry and promise to change their lives. Many of them hear God speak in their souls, "Your sins are as white as snow!" and they know peace, assurance, and love such as they've never known before.

One hundred million people tell someone, "Thank you," or "I'm sorry," or "I love you . . ." all at the same time. Right now. Here and now.

All of these examples are forms of prayer, handed down through the ages. Jesus told us to "pray always." The mystics taught us to see God all around us, to look for the Christ in each of us, and to listen for the Holy Spirit within ourselves. The saints taught us how to live. Catholic prayer is so much more than talking; it is listening, seeing, being, and doing.

The Catholic Church speaks of the "deposit of faith"—a phrase that points to the beliefs and practices deposited by men and women in Catholic consciousness for the past two thousand years. It's a spiritual vault so large and deep that no one can withdraw all of its riches in a thousand lifetimes. Some people think the phrase refers to a handful of doctrines or rules that others may doubt or disobey, but that's only part of it. The deposit of faith is not a limited checking account. It's a trust fund that increases and multiplies.

The varieties of Catholic prayer in the deposit of faith include the beautiful spiritual practices of the great religious orders. The earthy joy of the Franciscans. The disciplined rule of the Benedictines. The spiritual exercises of the Jesuits. The mysticism of the Carmelites. The simplicity of the Cistercians. The asceticism of the Dominicans. The care for the poor of the Little Sisters of the Poor. The mission work of the Maryknollers. And on and on. There are as many ways of "praying always" as there are ways of "living and moving and having our being in God."

Each kind of prayer uniquely manifests a quality of our loving God. They are all ways of entering into "conscious, loving communion with God," a common definition of prayer among theologians today.

We all participate in different forms of prayer at different times for different reasons. In *The Art of Praying*, Romano Guardini puts it this way: "There is prayer which responds to the remoteness of God—to His hiddenness and to His unknownness. Conversely, there is prayer which responds to His nearness, His openness, and His accessibility. There is prayer which springs forth from the direct comprehension of the truth—prayer which is, as it were, a spontaneous confession of faith. But there is also prayer which is a confession of ignorance, an admission of failure before the mystery. There is the prayer of plentitude, when God's presence is fully experienced; but there is also the prayer of privation when it appears that God has forsaken us, leaving a great void which nothing can fill. There are times when everything seems intelligible and familiar, and there are times when nothing seems to make sense or to be worthwhile, when there is no hope and no one to turn to—times when we must persevere in silence. All these different times demand their own forms of prayer."

Guardini names the basic forms of prayers as adoration, praise, thanksgiving, petition, intercession, and penance.

- Adoration and praise are spontaneous responses to God's greatness.
- Thanksgiving is a sincere gesture of gratitude.
- Prayers of petition and intercession seek the help of God for special favors.
- And penance reminds us of our human sinfulness.

It is not an accident that all forms of prayer can be found in the first and purest of all prayers, the Lord's Prayer:

Our Father, who art in heaven,
hallowed be thy name;
thy kingdom come;
thy will be done on earth
as it is in heaven.
Give us this day our daily bread;
and forgive us our trespasses,
as we forgive those that trespass against us;
and lead us not into temptation,
but deliver us from evil.
Amen.

The thirteenth-century Doctor of the Church Thomas Aquinas said, "The Lord's Prayer is the most perfect of prayers . . . In it we ask, not only for all the things we can rightly desire, but also in the sequence that they should be desired."

Catholics hold a "deposit of faith" that has been nurtured and sustained by Christian ancestors who, over the span of two millennia, have sought in every language—art, literature, dance, music, symbols, and gestures—to enter into conscious communion with Love. That is the variety—and the beauty—of Catholic prayer.

❧

The Brooklyn Dodgers and the Catholic Church
BY DORIS KEARNS GOODWIN

My early years were happily governed by the dual calendars of the Brooklyn Dodgers and the Catholic Church. The final out of the last game of the World Series signaled the approach of winter, bringing baseball hibernation, relieved only by rumors of trades and reports of contract negotiations. Even before the buds had appeared on the trees of Rockville Centre, players had sloughed off their winter weight and prepared to reconvene for spring training, bringing the joyous return of the box score (whose existence my father had finally revealed). Excitement mounted as the team returned to Brooklyn for opening day, a day of limitless promise. As spring yielded to summer, the pennant race began to heat up, reaching a peak of intensity—of mingled hope and apprehension—during the sultry days of August, when the hopes of many teams were still alive. By mid-September, a chill in the air of shortening days, the scales began to tip, depressing the hopes of many teams. For fans of contending teams, however, like the Dodgers of my childhood, it was Indian summer, a glorious respite before the last out of the last game opened the door once more to winter.

Analogous to the seasonal cycles of baseball were the great festivals of the Catholic Church. A month before Christmas we hung the Advent wreath, and each week we lit one of the four candles that presaged the coming of the Christ child. The fulfillment of Christmas followed, symbolized by the decoration of our Christmas tree, the exchange of gifts, and the mystery and wonder of Midnight Mass. When I was five or six, I would lie awake in bed, listening as the thunder of church bells at midnight announced the coming of the Savior, and dream of the day I would be permitted to stay up late enough to accompany my sisters to Midnight Mass. When I was finally allowed to go, none of my imaginings prepared me for the splendor of the church, its marble altars bordered with garlands of white and red poinsettias and dotted with red flames from clusters of small white candles surrounding the central one that symbolized Christ, the Light of the World. My parents worried that I wouldn't last through the two-hour service, but the sight of the altar, the priests' gold vestments, the sounds of the Latin ritual, and the soaring choir music overwhelmed fatigue until long after the service was completed.

The last weeks of winter brought Ash Wednesday and the beginning of Lent, commemorating the period of Jesus' fast in the desert. We knelt before the priest, who traced in ash the sign of the cross on our foreheads. "Remember," the priest intoned, his thumb touching each brow, "that thou art dust and unto dust shalt thou return." How much nearer death seemed to me when I was a child, when, kneeling like millions of other children, I said the nightly prayer: "Now I lay me down to sleep, I pray the Lord my soul to keep. If I should die before I wake, I pray the Lord my soul to take." But symbols of death were more than matched by symbols of rebirth, renewal, and resurrection, as the Lenten fast led up to Palm Sunday, marking the triumphal return of Jesus to Jerusalem. Holy Week— windows opening to the onrushing spring—continued through the solemnity of Holy Thursday and the deep mourning of Good Friday, when the church stood desolate and bare, its altar draped in black, its statues covered in purple, giving way to the joyful triumph of Easter Mass, when the church was bedecked in white lilies. As Easter had been preceded by forty days of sorrow, it was followed by fifty days of rejoicing, leading up to Whitsunday, the feast of the Pentecost, and the gift of the Holy Spirit. Through these seasonal festivals, so firmly embedded in the routine of our lives, I developed a lasting appreciation of the role that pageantry, ritual, and symbolism play in tying together the past and the present. . . .

So rich were the traditions and the liturgy of my church that I could not imagine being anything other than Catholic.

Doris Kearns Goodwin is a historian and the Pulitzer Prize–winning author of *No Ordinary Time.*

✧

What Makes Being Catholic Great?
A Child's Prayer
BY SUSAN HEYBOER O'KEEFE

What makes being Catholic great?
Lots of little things—
Incense, bells, and candles,
Feathery angel wings,
Stained glass in the morning,
A rosary to hold tight,
A priest up at the altar
In purple, green, or white.

What makes being Catholic great?
Lots of little things—
Playing with the Christmas crib,
The camels, and the kings,
Staying up for Midnight Mass
Long past the time for bed,
Skipping meat on Fridays
To have grilled cheese instead . . .

Dressing up like brides and grooms
On First Communion Day,
Making chains of daisies

For Mary's crown in May,
Drawing pictures of the saints
With halos shining bright,
Then helping fill up Noah's ark
With pets that never bite.

What makes being Catholic great?
Lots of big things, too—
Knowing Baby Jesus
Grew up like me and you,

Hearing how he saved us
By dying on the tree,
And now is always with us
As real as you or me . . .

Reading in the Bible
Good News for every day,
Finding full forgiveness
Those times we disobey,
Having seven sacraments
To mark the road ahead—
Like when a baby's baptized
Or a man and woman wed,
Seeing just one family
In every different face,
Winning life in heaven
To rest in God's embrace.

What makes being Catholic great?
Knowing it's so true
That God is good, and so are we,
And every day's brand new,
That every life's important,
And God loves each the same,

No matter our religion,
Our color, or our name.

I love being Catholic
Every single day!
It's how I show my love for God
In an extra special way.

The above is from a forthcoming picture book by **Susan Heyboer O'Keefe.** Her titles include *Angel Prayers, Countdown to Christmas, Sleepy Angel's First Bedtime Story,* and *Goodnight, God Bless.*

❧

Among the countless things I love about the Catholic faith are its many sacramentals. Sacramentals are sacred signs instituted by the church to remind us of God's loving presence. My rosary has taught me patience and fortitude; my prayerbook comfort through scripture and mental prayer; and my holy cards have taught me to hold on to and share the visual faith of our early ancestors.

Though it may strike some people as odd, my nun dolls have taught me how to mentor. When I look at my collection of dolls wearing their representative habits, I remember the women who made a difference in my life: St. Hildegard, St. Gertrude, St. Catherine of Siena, St. Teresa of Avila, and St. Thérèse of the Child Jesus. Without them I would have never known what it is like to sacrifice as a parent, teacher, wife, and budding entrepreneur. The nuns gave me themselves as mentors. They also gave me their founders. They have afforded me a way to mentor hundreds of students in a public community college in the desert of southern California.

> —Julie Ann Brown, professor of
> business (Antelope Valley College)
> Lancaster, California

Advent is my season. There is something about waiting in patience, in silence, for God to be born in me and in our world that seems to me to be the essence of what it means to be a woman pregnant with the Word, with a listening heart, an assenting heart. One Advent 15 years ago I was waiting for God to speak about my vocation. I had to wait, patiently, when I wanted him to speak loudly and clearly, or preferably, to send a postcard! One Advent more recently I was waiting for a "forgiveness baby" to gestate and be born in me. I could not hurry the process along, any more than a pregnant woman can force the child within her to grow and come to birth. Advent is "waiting on God time," when I realize more and more my dependency on God, and letting him be Lord of my life in his way.

—Sister Sheryl Chen, OCSO
Dubuque, Iowa

In Catholic grade school we were taught the devotion called the "Angelus." As a youngster it was pretty much a quiet prayer said as the church bells rang out at six in the morning, at noon, and again in the evening. But now, in later life, I realize that the Angelus is a beautiful summation of our spirituality: a) God's initiative as the angel declares to Mary the gift of the Spirit; b) our obedience, saying yes to God as Mary did; c) the enfleshment of the Word into history, an incarnation that we are to continue in our own day; and d) a concluding prayer which calls us to re-experience the paschal mystery, the life-death-resurrection of the Lord. In three minutes, three times a day, we can renew the dynamics of our spiritual lives.

—Robert F. Morneau,
Auxiliary Bishop
Green Bay, Wisconsin

I find that whenever I think about being Catholic, I naturally return to my grandmother. It was she who awakened and nurtured my faith by sharing her sense of belonging to a church community. My grandmother lived in a time and place when the church was the central institution in people's lives. She painted my imagination with stories of communal celebrations, patronal feasts, and cultural observances. She encouraged me to create my own memories within a community of faith. I grew up in a world of rituals and liturgical seasons. I also came to believe that being Catholic could only happen in community.

—Sister Yolanda Tarango, CCVI

San Antonio, Texas

⬥

Favorite Prayers

My favorite prayer is Proverbs 3:1–6. It gives the basic truths of what is expected of us and tells us how we should approach our God:

> *My son, forget not my teaching,*
> *keep in mind my commands;*
> *For many days, and years of life,*
> *and peace, will they bring you.*
> *Let not kindness and fidelity leave you;*
> *bind them around your neck;*
> *Then will you win favor and good esteem*
> *before God and man.*
> *Trust in the Lord with all your heart,*
> *on your own intelligence rely not;*
> *In all your ways be mindful of him,*
> *and he will make straight your paths.*

—Dave Wannstedt, football coach

Miami, Florida

One of my favorite prayers, probably a surprising one for a Franciscan, is a prayer of Saint Augustine. I first copied this prayer as a young college seminarian and affixed it to my mirror so that I could recite it every morning. Over the years it has been in my office book and now is kept at my prayer space. When I recite it, my world is again aligned, I have perspective, and God is in control.

"O Lord Jesus, let me know myself, let me know Thee, and desire nothing else but only Thee. Let me hate myself and love Thee, and do all things for the sake of Thee. Let me humble myself and exalt Thee, and think of nothing but only of Thee. Let me die to myself and live in Thee, and take whatever happens as coming from Thee. Let me forsake myself and walk after Thee, and ever desire to follow Thee. Let me turn from myself and turn to Thee, that so I may merit to be defended by Thee. Let me fear for myself, let me fear Thee, and be amongst those who are chosen by Thee. Let me distrust myself and trust in Thee, and ever obey for the love of Thee. Let me cleave to nothing but to Thee, and ever be poor for the sake of Thee. Look upon me, that I may love Thee; call me, that I may see Thee and forever possess Thee. Amen."

—Richard Rohr, O.F.M.,
author and retreat master
Albuquerque, New Mexico

I remember how, in parochial school, we used to invoke the names of Jesus, Mary, and Joseph, and we routinely wrote the initials "JMJ" on school papers. I still sometimes jot "JMJ" on my business notepads.

But besides formal prayers and Mass, the prayer I say most often is one I composed myself: "God, give me strength, help me make the right decision."

I say this prayer at least once a week, always before making any important decision. With all the problems of the business world and the challenges of everyday life, I am continuously prompted to turn to God for guidance.

—Robert Schwartz,
business executive

My favorite prayer is from Saint Teresa of Avila: "Christ has no body now but yours; no hands, no feet on earth, but yours. Yours are the eyes through which he looks with compassion on this world; yours are the feet with which he walks to do good; yours are the hands with which he blesses all the world. Christ has no body now on earth but yours."

—John Shea, theologian and storyteller
Chicago, Illinois

The rosary has helped me to lead a happy life devoted to the love of God and for the benefit of my family and my friends, and the welfare of my neighbor. . . . Some people might find the praying of the rosary silly, but for me, if I cannot sleep—if I am worried on a plane, if I am pacing the floor overwrought in thinking of my husband's illness—I hold the rosary in my hand, it gives me comfort, trust, serenity, a sense of understanding by the Blessed Mother because as I have talked and prayed to her all my life, in happy successful times, I know now she will understand and comfort me and bring me solace.

—Rose Fitzgerald Kennedy

✿

Two Classic Prayers

PRAYER OF SAINT FRANCIS

Lord, make me an instrument of Your peace.
Where there is hatred, let me sow love;
Where there is injury, pardon;
Where there is doubt, faith;
Where there is despair, hope;
Where there is darkness, light;
Where there is sadness, joy;

*O Divine Master, that I may
  seek
Not so much to be consoled as to
  console;
Not to be understood as to understand;
Not to be loved as to love;
For it is in giving that we receive;
It is in pardoning that we are
  pardoned;
And it is in dying that we are
  born to eternal life.*

PRAYER BY THOMAS MERTON

My Lord God, I have no idea where I am going. I do not see the road ahead of me. I cannot know for certain where it will end. Nor do I really know myself, and the fact that I think I am following your will does not mean that I am actually doing so. But I believe that the desire to please you does in fact please you. And I hope I have that desire in all that I am doing. I hope that I will never do anything apart from that desire.

And I know that if I do this you will lead me by the right road, though I may know nothing about it. Therefore I will trust you always though I may seem to be lost and in the shadow of death. I will not fear, for you are ever with me, and you will never leave me to face my perils alone.

My faith is extremely important to me and I'm not reluctant to tell my team that.

We publicly will talk about our sex lives, we publicly will talk about drug abuse, and we'll publicly talk about alcoholism, but you privately discuss your religion. I fight with myself about how much to put in, so I've made a decision that I am going to say things about religion as it pertains to me and let my players decide how to respond: "Hey, you know Coach said he heard the priest say something in church today." Well, he went to church. I'm not bragging about going to church as much as I want them to know that I need to go some place for strength.

And I think it's important for them to know that I am weak enough or I need the charging of my battery; I need to ask for help.

And I think we do need a little bit more of the traditional, formal type of religion brought out in our lives. You know, we have stricter religious laws than we have gun laws in the school system. That's really crazy.

Everybody's got to have a tool, a vehicle, a thing by which they negotiate the paths of life. I use basketball to do that because that's what God gave me and the tool I feel most comfortable with, obviously, because I went in that direction. But to use the ball as an end is a very foolish thing. That's what the deflation of it means.

To anybody who plays the game, a deflated basketball is a very depressing thing because you can do nothing else in the game with it. That's what I want to make them understand: Hey, if the air were let out of the ball, you still have got to have a value or purpose in your life in which you're trying to do it.

—John Thompson, basketball coach

Chapter Eight

EVERYONE CALLS ME FATHER . . .
OR SISTER . . . OR AL

Everybody Calls Me Father was a popular Catholic book in the 1950s. "You Can Call Me Al" was a popular song in the 1980s. Today a priest or a nun may like to be called Father or Sister or Al or Alice, but one thing is clear: Catholics respect and love them still. Indeed, many Catholics like to say, "Some of my best friends are priests and sisters." (Unless that Catholic is a priest or a sister; then they'll say, "Some of my best friends are lay people.") This chapter gives thanks not only to them but also to the good brothers and lay ministers who equally represent the "chosen part of things" to all of us.

I once asked one of my nieces, "Did you ever think of becoming a nun?" Her answer: "No, but I did think of becoming a priest."
—Andy Costello, CSSR
Lima, Ohio

"Dad, I think I have a vocation.
Dad, I want to become a nun!"

Sr. Miriam Therese Winter and her brothers and sisters

My calling is to be an authentic witness to faith. The people are telling us very clearly what they want. It is something very simple: Our presence with them. . . . This personal outreach is the heart of being a priest. Being present, even in simple ways, with the people is of vital importance.
—Cardinal Joseph Bernardin

I like being a Sister because I can be everybody's sister. It gives me the freedom to love everybody intensely and passionately. I can't imagine being anything else.
—Miriam Therese Winter,
Medical Mission Sister
Hartford, Connecticut

I like being a Brother because of the ways I can carry out my missionary ministry. A Brother is one whose vocation calls him to be rooted in service to his sisters and brothers in the human family through community, prayer and hospitality. Jesus, who is brother par excellence, is our example. He was with his friends, at meal, in prayer, and he washed their feet. A Brother is one who is challenged to call other men and women to the table, a round table, where all are equal. To me a Brother is not a title but a lifestyle in relation to others. Being a Brother is a gift from God, and I am grateful for it.

—Wayne Fitzpatrick, M.M.
Maryknoll, New York

When I was 17 years old, I "entered the convent." Seventeen years and one month later, I'm still "in the convent." (How many other lifestyles refer to entering and leaving buildings?) Granted, it's not the same convent—I've lived in five different convents since I "entered," not including novitiate mission experience and summer assignments—but I'm still here, or "in."

I know nothing about numerology, but does it count somewhere that I teach predominantly 17-year-olds? That is to say, when I'm not "in the convent," I'm usually at school.

I love it. I really enjoy the art of teaching, and sometimes I get it right. Sometimes I don't. But I love the Truth. Remember that great line in "Philadelphia" when Tom Hanks' character says, "I love the Law"? Yes, he definitely said it with a capital "L." And that's how I love the Truth. Right down to the bones. To teach a young person where he or she might begin to look for the Truth, and when searching, how to know what to look for, where it lurks, how to test it, and who may have already found it—that's the essence of good teaching I say.

My ever-inquisitive Juniors (the 17-year-olds) used to barrage me every afternoon with questions about religious life, a great diversion tactic from scanning iambic pentameter. I finally had to restrict their questions to two at the beginning of class, and only on Mondays. "Nundays" they call them. From not too probing: "Do you even wear that to bed?" to "Don't you ever just want to go out and have sex?" the questions come, two a week, the bravest kids primed by the more curious yet less articulate. The closest call for me was sometime during the Clinton-Dole debates: "Did you ever go to a concert when you were our age?" (Yes.) Followed by: "Did you ever do anything illegal while you were there?" (Well, yes.) Gasps, chuckles, knowing looks, conspiratorial camaraderie, elbows in the ribs, "betcha she didn't inhale" comments—(Yes, I concealed a recording device in my purse)—met with disappointed groans.

I can cover mostly anything they ask with a heartfelt "I've never done anything that God cannot forgive." (Hey, it was the 70's.)

—Claire King, S.C.C.

Madison, New Jersey

I like being a priest because, as a minister of the sacraments, I must find life in them in order to share that life with others at crucial moments in their lives. Preparation to lead others in prayer forces me to pray and to search for God in the day-to-day, the routines, and the ups and downs of human life.

—David E. Schlaver, C.S.C.

Phoenix, Arizona

I like being a Benedictine Sister because it taps every part of my personality. It immerses me in the contemplative and commits me to the world around me at the same time. It is a life of simple beauty and stable community and personal meaningfulness. It re-

Sr. Joan Chittister

Still Sr. Joan Chittister!

quires no mold and encourages personal development. It would be hard to find a life better than that.

—Joan Chittister, O.S.B.

Erie, Pennsylvania

I really owe so much to the Benedictines. They took me under their wing and realized I could sing. They put me in the big choir by the time I was 8 years old. I learned four-part Latin Masses and Gregorian chant. It was a wonderful training for me. I did that for 12 years.

—Florence Henderson, actress

Sister Fabian Reilly was an angel who believed that a musician, even one who played jazz, was a very good thing to be. I was always a little behind in my work because of my musical activities. When I was sent to the principal's office, she always arrived first to cop a plea for me. Whatever my problem, she could help me work it out.

"Just stick to your music," she said. "It's the best thing for you. You'll learn the other things."

—Woody Herman, jazz musician

I shocked my family when I told them of my desire to enter the seminary. My mother and sister cried. My brother laughed, and my father couldn't talk. This definitely wasn't the path I was destined to travel. My family lived the classic Korean-American experience. Hard work, good grades, responsibility, and balance were ingrained into our lives. Coupled with that was the deeply beautiful—our Catholic faith, loyalty to family, respect for elders, appreciation of tradition, value of culture, and most especially deep love—the kind that requires true depth of heart to understand.

Certainly, it took depth of heart for everybody, including myself, to understand my call to the priesthood. My siblings and I were all slated to take professional jobs, get married and provide our parents with the joy that comes with being grandparents. All my friends and relatives expected that. So, that's why I told most of them that I was getting married. I told them I was getting married to somebody they saw every week. In their utter shock, they tried unsuccessfully to name the person I was getting married to. It was kind of fun. It was even more fun delivering the second punch with the news that I was getting married to the Church.

Our souls are blessed with a "wild grace" as Catholic poet James Kirkup puts it. I guess mine is a bit wilder than my siblings, or maybe it's just weirder. Whatever the case, my crazy soul fell head-over-heals in love with Christ and his Church and ever since it has been the discovery adventure of a lifetime. That's the best part of being a seminarian—it's a grand learning experience filled with all the quirks and quandaries a young child makes in life. God is mystery and perfect love. Discovering his creation is humbling and awesome.

I thank the Lord for the wild grace of my soul, for without it, I don't think any person can be a whole-hearted Catholic, let alone a seminarian. Without it, one cannot possibly see the "dearest freshness deep down things" (Gerard Manley Hopkins).

As seminarians we are called to live a life of chastity, simplicity, and obedience, and we live in the middle of a world inundated with sex, money, and individualism. That's pretty wild. Christ in the eucharist, Christ in the poor, hungry, sick, and even in the enemy—that's deep stuff. And there have been some big mountains I've had to move in the course of my life. These are the deeply personal and deeply lovely triumphs I share with my family.

Today they support me with all their hearts. I will always be grateful to them.

—Eugene Justin Lee, seminarian
Orange, California

I like being a lay minister because you never know how God will call upon you to serve. How did a Jewish kid turned antitrust attorney end up teaching Bible study to adult Catholics? There really is room for all kinds under the big tent of the Catholic Church.

When I was baptized in 1976 at age 20, many of my agnostic friends thought I had gone crazy; when I quit being a lawyer to study in a Catholic lay ministry program in Seattle, they knew I had gone crazy! But I knew otherwise: the church today calls forth vocations to ministry of all kinds offered not only by priests and religious, but by married and single lay folks, too. So here I am, more than a decade later, a Bible teacher and writer, while my wife, Maggie, does part-time ministry as a spiritual director in a Jesuit spirituality program and as lay presider in our local parish. Who knows what ministry opportunities will await our son Peter, now in third grade at our parish school!

And what joy there is in pouring the living water of scripture on the sometimes parched desert of adult Catholics! Bible study was not part of many Catholics' upbringing, so most are fertile ground for the Word to grow in. There is little that brings me more true pleasure than seeing faith flower as nourished by the stories of our ancestors, whose journeys with God abound with hope and tragedy, humor and travail. God willing, I can imagine no better future than sharing these stories in the church until the day God calls me home.

—Wes Howard-Brook, lay minister
Seattle, Washington

I like being a bishop because I like being in community. I enjoy the second grader who, after we talked about school and baseball and being good to one another, raises his hand and asks, "How much do you know about God?"

I enjoy the coming together of the rich and poor, the educated and uneducated, the powerful and the weak into the same worship space, all mixed together.

—Robert F. Morneau, Auxiliary Bishop
Green Bay, Wisconsin

Being a priest who has served several parishes and religious communities over 50 years has put me in touch with the reality of the broad range of the people of God, for whom I was ordained to serve through preaching, teaching, and spiritual direction.

—Roland E. Murphy, O. Carm.,
biblical scholar
Washington, D.C.

There have been difficult days in my 55 years as a priest, but I can honestly say, not an unhappy day.

—John J. Egan
Chicago, Illinois

I like being a missionary even though mission overseas is marked by the pain, the loss, and the difficulties of the people with whom we work. But great joy also springs from the privilege of walking with those people, the poor of the developing world, in their daily struggle. Discovery is the most enriching and enjoyable part of mission. Each day in all the ordinary events of life the abundance of God's love breaks open. You find it in the companions you work with and in the people you serve—their willingness to help you learn the real meaning of life and the job of God's creation. I don't just like it, I love it!

—B. Peter Byrne,
Maryknoll missionary
Anaconda, Montana

Father Peter Byrne loves being a missionary

The Congregation of the Missionaries of Charity is only a small instrument in the

hands of God. We must take care that it stays that way, a little instrument. Very often I feel like a little pen in his hands. He's the one who thinks, writes, and acts; I am to be just a pencil, nothing more.

—Mother Teresa of Calcutta

When I was in grammar school with the nuns, they would tell stories and I would draw pictures of Christ on the cross. They loved it, and I would go show them to all the different nuns in all the different classes. They liked me a lot for some reason. First I

said I wanted to be a missionary—they *loved* that. One nun, Sister Gertrude in my third grade, she was terrific. "A missionary!" She'd slap me in the face because she liked it so much. "Ah! This boy! I love 'im." Either way, you got hit. "Ah, I love this boy!" Slap, slap, slap!

—Martin Scorsese, film director

Did you know that many of the religious priests, brothers, and sisters who gave their lives to give millions of Catholic schoolchildren a future now face an uncertain future? Religious communities of men and women are underfunded by several billions of dollars for retirement and health care. Out of hundreds of these communities in the United States, only a few are fully funded through charitable trusts for this purpose. Some groups could someday be put out on the streets. The annual parish collection for retired religious brings in more donations from Catholic parishioners than any other. Catholics are grateful for these heroic people who worked without material reward, but still it is not enough. If you're Catholic, the next time that collection comes around, you'll know what to do!

Just in Case You've Forgotten . . .

The Ten Commandments

1. I, the Lord, am your God. You shall not have other gods besides Me.
2. You shall not take the name of the Lord, your God, in vain.
3. Remember to keep holy the Sabbath day.
4. Honor your father and your mother.
5. You shall not kill.
6. You shall not commit adultery.
7. You shall not steal.
8. You shall not bear false witness against your neighbor.
9. You shall not covet your neighbor's wife.
10. You shall not covet anything that belongs to your neighbor.

The one commandment that threw me was "Thou shalt not covet thy neighbor's wife." Now I was seven and I always thought the priest was saying, "Thou do not *cover* your neighbor's wife." You can cover all the other wives in the neighborhood, and you're home free. But the minute you cover your neighbor's wife, you'd better get to confession.

—Bob Newhart

An Important Reminder . . .
Q: Where is God?
A: Everywhere

—*The Baltimore Catechism*

SAINTS PRESERVE US

The saints were your original stars, because you had their holy cards, you knew all their feast days.

—Marilu Henner, actress

Revisiting the saints year after year demonstrates and reinforces for me how we mere humans can live out the Christ-life in our diverse circumstances and know the company of a great cloud of witnesses on the Way.

—Walt Chura,
        teacher and retreat director
        Albany, New York

෴

Outrageous Holiness

BY ROSEMARY HAUGHTON

The saints—the canonized ones and the obscure ones—are one good reason to be a Catholic. One has to be a little selective—some saints were pushed to canonization by special interests and are best forgotten, but the undoubted evidence of real holiness in Catholic history is the one thing that has saved the church in the past and can do so now.

I became a Catholic at the age of 16—for all kinds of inadequate reasons, but at the heart of it was the attraction of that strange holiness. As a child, I read *Lives of the Saints for Children,* given to me by an Anglo-Catholic godmother. I read about people who did outrageous things I could only dream of: they ran away from home, disobeyed their parents, gave away their clothes, lived in caves, played with angels, nursed lepers! I daydreamed of such adventures, living in a private world of my own populated by these amazing people. But then I discovered that that world actually existed—it was to be found in the thing called Catholic.

I pursued it there. I found that holiness of even such outrageous kinds was still going on, and it was visible as it had always been visible, blazing through all the tawdry false pieties, stronger than the narrow spiritualities embraced, somehow even by the saints themselves, more enduring than patriarchal manipulation or worldly compromises.

The saints can be strange, often uncomfortable, stubborn, hard to get on with, even wrongheaded. But the compassion of Christ rages in them, Without that, there is no real church. With it, there is a reason to be Catholic.

Rosemary Haughton is one of the founders of Wellspring House, a shelter for homeless families in Gloucester, Massachusetts.

෴

I appreciate that the church has preserved and handed down the memory of its saints. Respect for the mystical tradition, especially, serves us well in this time of spiritual renewal. As we cast about for ways to awaken and name our deepest experiences of God, one another, and the earth, figures like Clare and Francis of Assisi, Hildegard of Bingen, Bernard of Clairvaux, Bonaventure, Julian of Norwich, Meister Eckhart, and Catherine of Siena are ready at hand. Such figures have always been part of our family, perhaps like eccentric aunts and uncles, who, although a bit weird, are regarded with affection and pride.

Mystics offer us a smorgasbord of words, images, and symbols that can serve us well as we broaden the horizons of what we understand by holiness to include all the baptized. The mystics cheer us on to grow in courage and compassion and love of neighbor.

—Elizabeth A. Dreyer,
professor of religious studies
(Fairfield University)
Hamden, Connecticut

Catholics find joy in what we call "the communion of saints." This means we belong to a community of faith that is not limited by time and space. Call it a fourth dimension, if you will; it is one that permeates the three dimensions we know through our senses. And through loving intimacy with God, we find ourselves participants in this community peopled by the countless souls who have gone before us in this work, all those now living and—from an eternal perspective, at least—all those who will be born in the centuries to come. What a mystery! What a joy!

—Mitch Finley, journalist and author
Spokane, Washington

I'm a big fan of St. Thomas More, and I keep next to the screen of my word processor a postcard of the Holbein from the Frick Museum, the famous portrait of Thomas More. And I keep it there for a reason: He keeps me straight. It's actually happened that when, in the course of doing a magazine piece or whatever, I'm tempted to fudge a quote—if I think, Well, this quote doesn't do exactly what I want it to do, so I'll just fix it up—then I look at More and I unfudge it.

—Christopher Buckley, author

Marlo Thomas describes her father's devotion to St. Jude:
My father [Danny Thomas] was a man of great faith. He made a promise to St. Jude in the early years of his career that if St. Jude would just give him a sign if he was going along the right way . . . and he said, "If I'm barking up the wrong tree, let me know. If this is what I should be doing, let me know."

And he put $7 in the church basket. And he said, "I have to have 10 times this." And that was on a Sunday. And the next day, Monday, he got a job for $75, playing a singing toothbrush in a radio commercial, and he took that as his sign.

He prayed to St. Jude all those years, and whenever I'd ask him anything, my Father would say, "Let me talk to St. Jude about it." And he made a promise to St. Jude: "If you guide me in my life, I will someday build you a shrine. . . ." So he decided to build St. Jude Children's Research Hospital, which he founded, which he thought of himself, which he raised the money himself, and maintained until he died.

While we're inspired by the physical and intellectual strength of our sports heroes, strength comes in different packages. Mother Teresa had great resolve and commitment, and while we can't all be nuns or priests, that doesn't mean we can't be a strong influence wherever we are. We don't have enough people now saying, "What I want to do is be a good person because I'm being tested for salvation."

—Frank Layden, basketball coach
Salt Lake City, Utah

St. Anthony of Padua

St. Catherine of Bologna

St. Christopher

I like being Catholic because of the saints. Sometimes God seems so unapproachable. Saints are not only role models you can relate to, you can approach them for different needs. You lose something, you go to St. Anthony. You need a compassionate code to live by, you go to St. Francis. And if it all seems hopeless, there's always St. Jude.

St. Joan of Arc

—Guy Giarrizzo,
theater director
New York City

St. Jude the Apostle

St. Lucy

St. Joseph

❧

Ten Catholic Heroes of the Twentieth Century
BY ROBERT ELLSBERG

One of the distinctive traditions of Catholicism is the naming and vener-ation of saints. These are not perfect or super-people. They are simply men and women whose lives, in some measure, remind us of the holiness of Christ. Drawing on their example, we may be inspired to respond more faithfully to our own vocation to holiness. For ultimately—so the church teaches—that is the vocation of all of us: to put off the old man or woman and put on Christ.

There is a tendency to think of saints as people of long ago. Because the process of canonization is long and complicated there are relatively fewer official saints from our recent past. But the twentieth century has seen no shortage of heroic Christian witnesses. What follows is a list of ten—not the "top ten"—but simply ten great Catholics from the past century. They are not proposed as "patron" saints for a partic-ular group or cause. Rather than turn to any one person of the past, I find myself drawing on some saints who help me to be more coura-geous; some who help me to be more forgiving; some who help me over-come my fear of looking like a fool. Here are ten Catholic men and women who have enlarged my understanding of what it means to be a human being.

1. *Charles de Foucauld (1858–1916): Desert Hermit.* As a youth this French aristocrat seemed suited for little beyond a life of idleness and self-indulgence. But after an astonishing conversion he pursued his vocation with single-minded focus. The turning point in his life came with a pilgrimage to the Holy Land and the opportunity to visit the actual sites where Christ had spent his life. He was struck by the in-sight that Jesus, though the Son of God, had spent most of his life as a humble carpenter in an obscure village in Galilee. This became the foundation for his own vocation. First in Nazareth itself, and then

among the Muslim nomads of North Africa, he set out to emulate the "hidden life" of Jesus, proclaiming the gospel not simply by words but by his life of prayer and humble service. By the time of his death in 1916 he had attracted no followers. Years later, however, his spiritual legacy was claimed by several congregations and countless lay people, all inspired by his example of contemplative witness in the midst of the world.

2. *Dorothy Day (1897–1980): Founder of the* Catholic Worker. As a child, Dorothy Day exulted in the lives of the saints and their stories of heroic charity. But where, she asked, were the saints to change the

social order—not simply to minister to its victims? Her passion for social justice led her to join forces with the communists and other radicals. But the experience of bearing a child awakened a thirst for God that ultimately led her into the Catholic church. The struggle to find some way of reconciling her new faith with her social commitments was answered by her encounter with Peter Maurin, a French peasant-philosopher. Inspired by his "personalist" vision, in 1933 she launched the *Catholic Worker*, a newspaper and movement devoted to proclaiming and living out the radical social implications of the gospel. Beginning in New York's Lower East Side, she established houses of hospitality for the practice of the "works of mercy." What we do for the poor, she wrote, we do directly for Jesus. At the same time she challenged the structures of injustice and the habits of indifference responsible for so much need and misery. A consistent pacifist, she was arrested numerous times for her protests against war. Though her political views put her far outside the mainstream, by the time of her death in 1980 she was revered by many as the heart and conscience of the American Catholic Church.

3. *Franz Jagerstatter (1907–1943): Martyr of Conscience.* This simple farmer was the single Catholic layman executed in Austria for refusing to serve in the Nazi army. As remarkable as his solitary witness is the fact that he took his stand against the counsel of several priests as well as his local bishop. All of them told him that his duty as a Catholic was to serve his country, obey the law, and leave higher moral discernment to those in authority. His own conscience instructed him otherwise. Believing that any compromise with the Nazi cause was a mortal sin, he freely submitted to death. He was beheaded in 1943, leaving a wife and three daughters. For years his memory was an embarrassment to his neighbors and the church of his homeland. Increasingly, however, he is honored as a martyr of conscience, whose courageous witness helped to redeem a dark era.

4. *Pierre Teilhard de Chardin (1881–1955): Mystic and Scientist.* This French Jesuit was a courageous pioneer in the effort to reconcile the languages of science and faith. His professional life as a geologist and paleontologist was spent uncovering the secrets of evolution and human origins. All the while he was afire with a profoundly mystical vision of the divine mystery at the heart of the cosmos. In scores of books and essays he labored on a theological synthesis, integrating the theory of evolution with his own cosmic vision of Christianity. The

Vatican, suspicious of his project, forbade Teilhard from teaching or publishing any of his writings throughout his lifetime. Only after his death in 1955 was his work known beyond a small circle of Jesuit friends. It is that work that has linked Teilhard's name to many of the most hopeful and creative movements in contemporary theology and spirituality.

5. *Pope John XXIII (1881–1963): A Pope for All Seasons.* Pope John XXIII was seventy-seven at the time of his election in 1958. Though he presented a jolly contrast to his somewhat imperious predecessor, there was little doubt that his would be a "transitional" papacy, filling the chair of Peter until the next conclave. Instead Pope John offered a much more radical transition, bridging two eras in the history of the church. Soon after his election he stunned the world by announcing plans for a general church council, only the second such gathering since the sixteenth century. Not only did Pope John convene the Second Vatican Council, but he set its tone and agenda. Speaking of the need for the church to "open the windows," he initiated a new era of openness and positive dialogue between the church and the modern world. When he died in 1963 the work of the Council was still in progress. But in a few short years Pope John had established a new model of pastoral and prophetic leadership, and thereby won the hearts of the world.

6. *Thomas Merton (1915–1968): Monk.* The publication in 1948 of Thomas Merton's autobiography, *The Seven Storey Mountain,* made him the most famous monk in America. With great poignancy, he told the story of his restless youth, his conversion to Catholicism, and his decision, on the eve of World War II, to enter the strict enclosure of a Trappist monastery in Kentucky. But that was not the end of his story. Much later, after years as a monk, he would describe an experience of mystical insight that occurred during a visit to Louisville. Looking at all the people in a downtown intersection he experienced a sense of intense solidarity with the human race: "There are no strangers! . . . The gate of heaven is everywhere." Though he remained

committed to his monastic vocation, no longer did he see the monastery as an escape from "the world," but as a place of prophetic witness and loving service. His later books reflected a balance between contemplative prayer and openness to the world that became the distinctive feature of his spirituality. Since his death in 1968 his many writings have continued to connect the ancient wisdom of the Christian tradition with the spiritual yearnings of modern readers.

7. *Oscar Romero (1917–1980): Archbishop and Martyr.* For most of his life, Oscar Romero pursued an unremarkable ecclesiastical career. In 1977, when he was named archbishop of San Salvador, his reputation as a pious and conservative bishop endeared him to El Salvador's entrenched oligarchy. But by then the country's deep social conflicts were rapidly reaching a crisis point. Soon after his consecration, Romero was shocked by the murder of one of his priests, an outspoken champion of social justice. Suddenly awakened to the social dimensions of the gospel, Romero underwent an astonishing conversion. He became the embodiment of the prophetic church, a "voice of the voiceless," and a courageous defender of the poor. "On this point," he said, "there is no possible neutrality. We either believe in a God of life or we serve the idols of death." After three short years Romero was himself assassinated as he said Mass. It was a death he freely accepted, confident that "a bishop will die, but the church of God—the people—will never die."

8. *Mother Teresa of Calcutta (1910–1997): Foundress of the Missionaries of Charity.* Long before her death in 1997 Mother Teresa was revered as a living saint. Her famous ministry to the dying and discarded poor of Calcutta earned her every honor and recognition, including the Nobel Peace Prize. All this was in marked contrast to the obscurity of her beginnings. In 1946, when she took up her work with the poor, she was a thirty-six-year-old Loretto sister who had spent the previous twenty years teaching middle-class students in her order's schools in India. One day she received a call from God: "He wanted me to be poor with the poor and to love him in the distressing disguise of the poorest of

the poor." It was only after decades of such toil that she was "discovered" by the world. Even then she remained remarkably unaffected by adulation. She challenged others to take their own small steps in love. "To show great love for God and our neighbor we need not do great things. It is how much love we put in the doing that makes our offering something beautiful for God."

9. *Bede Griffiths (1906–1994): Pilgrim to the East.* Bede Griffith's journey to God was a classic story of the spiritual encounter between East and West. The first half of his adult life was spent as a monk in England. In 1955 he traveled to southern India to establish a Christian monastery there. In the ancient religious culture of India he was indelibly impressed by what he called "a sense of the sacred." The secularized West, he came to believe, had much to learn from India. Increasingly his mission was to witness the "marriage of East and West," attempting to facilitate an encounter between Western rationality and the intuitive spirituality that remained a part of Indian soul. He took up yoga, meditation, and other Indian spiritual disciplines. He immersed himself in Hindu classics, and in other ways adapted his monastery to Indian culture. In his old age he looked every bit the part of an Indian holy man—with long beard, flowing white hair, and saffron robe. Yet he remained thoroughly rooted in Christianity. He had come to the point where all religions, indeed all creation, spoke to him of God. For many in this era of "interreligious dialogue," he was a holy guide and guru.

10. *Joseph Cardinal Bernardin (1928–1996): Archbishop of Chicago.* By his later years, Joseph Bernardin, the archbishop of Chicago, was commonly described as the leader of the American Catholic Church. His ecclesiastical career included terms as the first general secretary and later president of the National Conference of Catholic Bishops. As archbishop of Cincinnati in the early 1980s he had overseen the drafting of the bishops' courageous pastoral letter on peace. Later he won wide praise for articulating what we called a "seamless garment" approach to the sacredness of life—broadening the church's pro-life

stance on abortion to encompass similar concern about capital punishment, euthanasia, and other forms of violence. These were among his achievements as a distinguished churchman. But it was more in the personal realm, in his embodiment of faith, hope, and charity, that he achieved his true pastoral leadership, and so came to be regarded as a true man of God. His final years were marked by a series of ordeals that constituted a veritable way of the cross. First came a false accusation of sexual misconduct. His accuser, a troubled young man dying of AIDS, ultimately withdrew his charges and in turn received the Cardinal's forgiveness. Then came Bernardin's very public journey with the cancer that ultimately took his life. Though he acknowledged his sufferings and his fears he welcomed death as "a friend," and so offered a Christian lesson in dying—and living—that touched the world.

11. *Honorable Mention: Flannery O'Connor (1925–1964): Novelist.* Traditionally the official list of saints has suggested that the common path to holiness has been by way of the convent or monastery. The number of "lay saints" is woefully limited. And yet the church has acknowledged that the call to holiness is for everyone, regardless of status or station in life. One woman who might well be added to the list is Flannery O'Connor, a Southern writer who rarely strayed from her

mother's farm in Milledgeville, Georgia, and who died at the age of thirty-nine of a debilitating disease. Unlike most "Catholic writers," she avoided Catholic settings in her stories. And yet, she wrote, "I write the way I do because (not though) I am a Catholic." Her sense of reality was indelibly stamped by the doctrine of the Incarnation; all her stories were about "the action of grace on a character who is not very willing to support it." O'Connor's posthumously published letters not only revealed the religious dimension of her darkly comic stories but also showed how the author's circumscribed life provided the arena for her own spiritual ascent. She saw the world and valued it in the light of eternity—which is to say, in all its precious contingency.

Robert Ellsberg, editor-in-chief of Orbis Books, is author of the best-selling *All Saints: Daily Reflections on Saints, Prophets, and Witnesses for Our Times.*

INTERLUDE

Martin E. Marty, Pulitzer Prize–winning church historian, describes him-self as "a Lutheran Christian, and thus an evangelical catholic." He also writes frequently and appreciatively about Catholics, and thus deserves a place in this book as an honorary Catholic.

I like being a "Catholic" for etymological reasons. *Catholic* comes from *kata* and *holos*, and means "relating to the whole." I wel-come an accent on the fact that Christian faith penetrates every dimension of being. It allows for "pan sacramentalism" in relation to arts, politics, friendship, and other good, if ambitious, things in the created order. One can have a good time with bread and wine and a Great time with The Bread and The Wine.

—Martin E. Marty, church historian
Chicago, Illinois

The Latin Church, which I find myself admiring more and more despite its frequent, astounding imbecilities, has always kept clearly before it the fact that religion is not a syllogism but a poem.

—H. L. Mencken

I really don't discuss religion or my beliefs. But when Stanley [Kubrick] died, I had an extraordinary night. I actually went out alone to St. Patrick's Cathedral and spent an hour and a half in the church. It was candlelit, the wind was whipping around that night, and I left at nine, when they close the doors. I thought as I came onto the street: *Well, I suppose once a Catholic, always a Catholic*. It was very humbling. I received such solace.

—Nicole Kidman, actress

THE GREAT COMMANDMENT

When the Pharisees heard that [Jesus] had silenced the Sadducees, they gathered together, and one of them, a lawyer, asked him a question to test him. "Teacher, which commandment in the law is the greatest?" He said to him, " 'You shall love the Lord your God with all your heart, and with all your soul, and with all your mind.' This is the greatest and first commandment. And a second is like it: 'You shall love your neighbor as yourself.' On these two commandments hang all the law and the prophets."
—Matthew 22:34–40

CORPORAL WORKS OF MERCY

1. Feed the hungry
2. Give drink to the thirsty
3. Clothe the naked
4. Visit the imprisoned
5. Shelter the homeless
6. Visit the sick
7. Bury the dead

※

The Challenge of Stewardship

BY MARIO CUOMO

Ours was a Catholicism closer to the peasant roots of its practitioners than to the high intellectual traditions of Catholic theology and philosophy. We perceived the world then as a sort of cosmic basic training course, filled by God with obstacles and traps to weed out the recruits unfit for eventual service in the Heavenly Host. At this, God had been exceedingly successful: the obstacles were everywhere. Our fate on earth was to be "the poor banished children of Eve, mourning and weeping in this vale of tears," until by some combination of luck and grace and good works, we escaped final damnation.

I don't mean to belittle the church of that time. Indeed, it was not the church so much as it was we churchgoers. Our faith reflected the collective experience of people who through most of their history had little chance to concern themselves with helping the poor or healing the world's wounds. They *were* the poor. Their poverty and their endless—sometimes losing—struggle to feed themselves and hold their families together had varied little across the centuries.

But what I now un-

derstand is that, in those days, in our preoccupation with evil and temptation, we often put guilt before responsibility and we obscured a central
part of Christian truth: that God did not intend this world only as a test
of our purity but, rather, as an expression of his love. That we are meant
to live actively, intensely, totally in this world and, in so doing, to make it
better for all whom we can touch, no matter how remotely.

So for people like me, struggling to believe, my Catholic faith and the
understanding it gives me of stewardship aren't a part of my politics.
Rather, my politics is, as far as I can make it happen, an extension of this
faith and the understanding.

I think my religion encourages me to be involved in government because it is very much a part of the world God so loves. And I think that if I
am given the burdens and the opportunities of stewardship, my principal
obligation is to use government not to impose a universal oath of religious
allegiance, or a form of ritual, or even a life style, but to move us toward the
shared commitments that are basic to all forms of compassionate belief.

Teilhard de Chardin in just a few magnificent sentences captured
everything I've tried to say here about this challenge of stewardship.
Talking about our obligations to involve ourselves in the things of this
world, he wrote: "We must try everything for Christ . . . Jerusalem, lift up
your head. Look at the immense crowds of those who build and those who
seek. All over the world, men are toiling—in laboratories, in studios, in
deserts, in factories—in the vast social crucible. The ferment that is taking
place by their instrumentality in art and science and thought is happening
for your sake. Open, then, your arms and your heart, like Christ your
Lord, and welcome the waters, the flood and the sap of humanity. Accept
it, this sap—for without baptism, you will wither, without desire, like a
flower out of water; and tend it, since, without your sun, it will disperse
itself wildly in sterile shoots."

And Jesus, answering the question of a lawyer in language to be understood by all, said that the law and the prophets, their wisdom and vision and insight, their teaching about religious obligation and stewardship, were all contained in two commandments: "You shall love the Lord
your God with all your heart, and with all your soul, and with all your
mind. You shall love your neighbor as yourself."

That is the law, as simply as it can be expressed—for both the stewards and those in their charge, for both the governed and those who govern them, for all who look to Christ's mercy, wherever they might find themselves.

Mario Cuomo is the former governor of New York.

❧

One Little Action at a Time
BY PATRICIA CROWLEY

It was not the 6:30 A.M. daily mass routine, nor was it the family rosary on our knees after dinner that did it. It was memories of delivering boxes of Christmas food and gifts to families who lived in poverty and it was also the family praxis of observe, judge, and act that stretched my young heart and mind and challenged me to probe more deeply into the social justice message of the gospel.

My parents were special people named Pat and Patty Crowley. They helped found the Christian Family Movement (CFM) and that movement defined their lives, their relationships with others, and their faith from 1948 (when I was 9 years old) on. The movement spread like a million angels of love and service throughout the world in the 50s and 60s. My parents were the lead couple and our house was the CFM office for many years.

Not only as their child but as a child of the times, I was blessed to grow up in a church that was searching for new ways to understand its doctrine and its liturgy and itself. When I was four years old, Pius XII published a document that was formative in my parents' lives and subsequently in mine—the encyclical *Mystici Corporis*, the Mystical Body of Christ. I remember my friends telling me how they wondered about their parents' admonishment to eat all their food because there were starving children in China. Now, my parents never used that particular motivational force but I do believe that I really did understand that if there were starving children anywhere, our lives were definitely connected. After all,

A future Benedictine with her parents, Pat and Patty Crowley

weren't we all one Body and, if one part hurt, of course, the other parts felt it!

I grew up in a house that welcomed people from all over the world, people of every color, culture and country. It was the norm to have several continents represented at our dinner table each night. We knew families of all economic strata and all racial backgrounds. I never thought about their being less than I!

In my formative years the great social encyclicals around labor and peace were being touted as the norm. We were at peace from the time I was six until my adolescence and then again in my young adulthood. No one in my immediate family was hurt or killed in any war. With all my heart, I believed in peace; I believed in justice for all workers and those beliefs, I know, were rooted in the social doctrine of the church proclaimed so clearly by my parents.

As I moved into my mid-twenties, the chaos of the 1960s broke loose in my ordered world: with wars that seemed senseless, with unexpected assassinations that frightened me, with revelations of unbelievable racial discrimination and injustice, with students being killed because they were part of a protest, etc., etc., etc. At the very same time, my church was going through a major transformation. For me, this was very hopeful in the midst of chaotic changes that were so evident in the society in which I lived.

As I reached my third decade, my parents' experience of that church began to change through their truly life-altering experience on the Birth Control Commission that preceded the publication of *Humanae Vitae*. As they were experiencing that "upset," I was deeply engrossed in the study of theology and was becoming more and more involved in some of the great social movements of the Catholic Church of our century.

In the next two decades, I was blessed to be a part of many different actions and groups that gave me a new sense of life and that deepened my love and appreciation of the breadth and the depth of the Catholicism on which I had been raised. One example of this occurred in 1980 as we Benedictines celebrated our 1500th anniversary (our "sesquimillennium"!). We came together for a week of reflection and for "peace actions" at the Pentagon. Out of that event, was born Benedictines for Peace, which continues to focus each of our communities on peace and justice. With that group we organized to support the publication of the Peace Pastoral by the American Bishops.

Later in that decade, through the National Assembly of Religious Women (N.A.R.W.), the vibrant movement of Catholic women concerned about social justice and led by the indomitable Marjorie Tuite, O.P., I traveled to Central America for the first time and there, in the midst of civil war, with a dozen or so North American and Latin American women, reflected and prayed and served and learned. This experience led me to my most significant experience of the living church wherein some 100 different women organized themselves into a living "sanctuary" to welcome a Salvadoran family into our midst. An amazing bonding occurred in that process. I resonated, once again, with the very real power of "being church," a power I had learned well from my parents.

So, with all of this, how could I not like being Catholic? I love being Catholic.

I ask myself, how in the midst of the turmoil of our church and of religious life specifically, I can honestly say that I do love being Catholic. As I do so, I come up with many good possibilities which I set forth here in the form of questions: Is it perhaps that call to social justice and the connectedness of all human beings which I learned so early in life? Is it perhaps the strong women mentors and models I learned of as a child: Catherine of Siena, Thérèse of Lisieux, Teresa of Avila, Dorothy Day, Catherine DeHueck Doherty?

Or is it the strong tradition of work for peace and justice?

Is it the expansiveness of Catholicism?

Is it the marvelous liturgical celebrations that we, as Catholics, are privileged to experience?

Is it the innate sense of struggle and the search for God and for truth that is so evident in the history of the church and her people throughout the world?

I do believe that it is all of the above. I enjoy the struggle, the expansiveness, the sense of journey, the strong feminine models, the holiness of many of its people, the liturgy, the theology, the genuine search for God, the contemplative path, and so much more.

I know one thing, that through all the struggles that I (we) face daily in this church we call "catholic," I never doubt that, though there are parts of this church that do not make sense or touch my heart, this is my church and that this is where I belong. I learned well from the church that I am church, that we are the church and that the church is the people of God. In that great tradition of peace and justice that I learned as a child, that I witnessed alive in Latin America and that I continue to grow in each day as an adult, I rejoice that I am a Catholic.

Patricia Crowley, O.S.B, is the executive director of Deborah's Place, a not-for-profit organization in Chicago providing shelter, supportive housing, and services to women who are homeless or formerly homeless.

◈

Whether I deliver lunch to someone in need, decorate a cake for someone I love, or kneel quietly before an array of burning long-stem candles in a church half a world away, I act as a Catholic. And I am inspired to do so much more after I read or hear about other Catholics performing great acts of service and kindness.
—Sue Fox McGovern
Park Ridge, Illinois

I like being Catholic because of the rich tradition of effort on behalf of social justice. This tradition goes back, of course, to the essence of the Gospel, but I also take particular strength from the example of leaders closer to our own time, such as Dorothy Day, Peter Maurin, and Jesuits Daniel Berrigan and John Dear. A key element to this experience of Catholicism has been an emphasis on our shared humanity with all people—a recognition that our concept of "neighbor" must be all-encompassing, not limited by physical proximity, faith, culture, ethnicity, gender, or economic status. I take pride in and strength from the lineage of those people who have lived this message, offering not ideology, but themselves.

—Trace Murphy,
editor
New York, New York

As a young adult Catholic, one of the most important contributions that the faith of the church has made to my life is its commitment to justice and solidarity with the oppressed. Throughout the past 10 years I have had the opportunity to work with different Catholic organizations or individuals that take seriously this aspect of our faith tradition. Creighton University initiated me through a multitude of service opportunities, including a summer program in the Dominican Republic, where I worked in a medical clinic and lived with a poor family. After graduating I spent a year in the Jesuit Volunteer Corps (JVC), where I lived in an intentional faith community of young adults and worked with poor, undocumented immigrants from Central America. The JVC claims that when you finish your year you will be "ruined for life." This is appropriate, because once you spend a year living among and working directly with the poor, or on their behalf, you will be profoundly changed.

I now have the opportunity to teach undergraduate courses on poverty and the Catholic tradition. As part of the course, I assign so many hours of community service. Many of my students tell me that they will continue the service work once the course is completed. They too are learning that by following the prophetic tradition within Catholicism, which seeks justice and lives in solidarity with the poor and oppressed, one will struggle and be "ruined for life."

—Liz Collier, twenty-nine years old,
student and teacher
Chicago, Illinois

The Catholic Church gives me a global religious community with a two-thousand-year tradition that situates me in space and time and calls me to work toward the realization of God's reign on earth.

—Joseph Martos
Louisville, Kentucky

I like being Catholic because the church's teaching on social justice makes me proud to be a member. Whether it's embodied in a papal pronouncement, a Catholic Worker house of hospitality or recent college graduates choosing to do a year of service, I find myself amazed and impressed by the church's care for the dignity of the human person and especially for the poor. I often say Catholic social teaching is the church's best-kept secret—one I wish weren't so secret. When other things about the church bother me, I can always count on this aspect of Catholicism to keep me from getting too cynical.

—Heidi Schlumpf, editor
Chicago, Illinois

When discussing the important influences in my life, I usually begin with the church, which teaches that true and great compassion means doing everything possible to alleviate every kind of suffering.

—Louis Freeh, FBI director

When I was in politics I never found it a problem to be there with my Roman Catholic faith. It also has to do with an interpretation of history and religion. I see that people are on the way to the end of time, and the Lord who has created the world is at the end of time, inviting us.

—Ruud Lubbers,
former Dutch prime minister

If I have an ability to do good for faith and religious tolerance, as a member of Congress, that's where my passion should be—concrete things that I feel I can do. Whether it's releasing prisoners or trying to bring nations together that have deep divisions, or protecting sacred sites, I think that's how I wish to express my faith.

—Bill Richardson, former congressman
from New Mexico, Secretary of Energy

I like being Catholic because I am joyful, grateful, and assured.
—David D. Fosca, school bus driver
Tucson, Arizona

I love the small "c" of Catholicism. When my local church gathers for worship, I see whites, blacks, Latinos and Asians, young and old, rich and poor. The homeless are welcomed as well as professional people, able people as well as the mentally and physically disabled. And I know that this wonderful universality, with its promise of human unity across every barrier that divides, will happen again and again as Mass is celebrated continually around the world.
—Richard K. Taylor
Philadelphia, PA

Authentic Catholicism entails being unafraid of anything since all aspects of human history and culture—human artifacts, music and art, cultural practices, intellectual masterpieces—may be stirrings of the Spirit of God who is bringing about the salvation of the world. Catholicism, which means "the whole," is the belief in the power of the Holy Spirit to unify peoples and cultures across space and time without obliterating what is distinctive to each.
—Catherine Mowry LaCugna,
theologian

The thing I like about being Catholic is that I feel like I belong. I like having a base.
—Claire Catanese, innkeeper,
Barclay Cottage,
Virginia Beach, Virginia

———————⚜———————

Chapter Eleven

CATHOLIC CULTURE—
IT'S EVERYWHERE

The Catholic ethos runs through Western culture like gold through a moun-
tain range. Catholic culture is like Catholicism itself: universal, diverse, and
painted with rainbow colors. It's as deep as a catacomb and as high as a
cathedral—low brow, high brow and everything in-between. It embraces
Michelangelo and Andy Warhol, Flannery O'Connor and Mario Puzo,
Mozart and Alanis Morisette. Catholic culture is 2,000 years old, sprinkles
every art form with stardust, and is just getting started.

    This modest chapter offers a taste, just a taste, of the Catholic ethos found
in popular culture: books, movies, and music. It's meant to be fun: You'll surely
want to add to and subtract from the examples given. Ever mindful of the old
Latin truism—"De gustibus non disputandum"—we invite you to sip from
our cup!

> *Where e'er the Catholic sun doth shine*
> *There's music and laughter and good red wine.*
> *At least I've always found it so,*
> *Benedicamus Domino!*
>
>   —Hilaire Belloc, author and poet

I believe that what I do is part and parcel of my spiritual journey. I believe acting has a spiritual resonance in my life. For
anybody who's an artist, and I hope that I'm not presumptuous
in calling myself an artist, work has a spiritual significance. If

you make shoes and make them with love, it has spiritual significance.

—Mercedes Ruehl, actress

When people have told me that because I am a Catholic, I cannot be an artist, I have had to reply, ruefully, that because I am a
Catholic I cannot afford to be less than an artist.

—Flannery O'Connor, novelist

~✤~

The Ten Best Catholic Novels You'll Ever Read
BY PATRICK SAMWAY

In much the same way that I am not sure that Catholic mathematics or
Catholic watercolors exist, so too I am not sure about putting too much
stock in the category of "Catholic novels." I do know that there are
Catholic authors who write novels, but can we call their novels
"Catholic"? Since the word Catholic is not under copyright, what does it
mean exactly? Should the definition of Catholic be restricted to someone
who has been baptized in a Roman Catholic church? Or is more at stake?
What do you call someone baptized in this church but who no longer believes what the Roman Catholic Church teaches? Can a novel by such a
person be called a "Fallen-Away Catholic Novel"? And is there such a creature as a "Uniate Catholic Novel"?

By posing such questions, I merely want to open up—and not restrict—any discussion about Catholic novels, particularly in suggesting
that, in my view, it might be legitimate to call a novel Catholic/catholic if
it dramatizes a view of the world that provides an opportunity for the
reader to enter in some reflective way into the mysterious plan that God
has for his people. Given this, let me make a few suggestions.

1. *The Power and the Glory,* by Graham Greene. I remember seeing the
play version of this novel on Broadway many years ago and over-

hearing an elderly Irish woman comment as we exited the theater, "Oh, now, they shouldn't do that to a priest of God." Since the death of English-born Graham Greene (1904–91) in Switzerland, it seems that his literary stock has remained constant. *The Power and the Glory* focuses on Father Montez, an alcoholic priest who has fathered a child at a time when anti-Catholic forces exerted considerable influence in Mexico. This priest serves as an anti-hero who, in spite of his

tremendous failures, does not deny his faith or his fellow Catholics when it counts most.

2. *Absalom, Absalom!* by William Faulkner. I consider this to be one of the truly great novels in English of the 20th century. Though Faulkner was not a Catholic (in fact, it would be difficult to make a case that he was a Christian), he did deal explicitly with the Christ-story in his novel *A Fable. Absalom, Absalom!* based on episodes found in the Old Testament (2 Samuel 7) seeks to find out the truth about a man who pursues his own self-aggrandizement at the cost of destroying those around him.

3. *Ulysses,* by James Joyce. By proposing this novel, I might be on safer ground. Joyce was baptized a Roman Catholic and educated in Jesuit schools before he sought exile from his past. In *Ulysses,* Joyce pushed the form of the novel to its limit, and in doing so provided traps for meditation as we follow Leopold Bloom in his journeys around

Dublin. If this novel proves too formidable, then I suggest Joyce's *A Portrait of the Artist as a Young Man.*

4. *The Last Gentleman,* by Walker Percy. Perhaps because I wrote a biography of Dr. Percy and have a great affection for his fiction and non-fiction, I highly recommend this novel about a young man searching for answers to pressing problems about life. It is not by chance that he ends up in Santa Fe, New Mexico—the City of Holy Faith.

5. *The Lieutenant,* by Andre Dubus. The author, who passed away in 1999, is not by reputation a novelist. My reason for listing this particular novel is that, among contemporary Catholic writers, Dubus holds a special place, precisely because of his commitment to his faith, which informs his fiction and gives it depth and honesty. Since he is at heart a writer of novellas, I highly recommend his *Selected Stories.*

6. *Wise Blood,* by Flannery O'Connor. Like Dubus, O'Connor mastered the story form—in her case, of stories that encapsulated the essential mysteries of the Catholic (and Protestant) faith. At times, it is possible to feel while reading an O'Connor story that it emerges from some type of spiritual equation that can only really be solved by prayerful reflection. I would be totally remiss if I did not mention her *Complete Stories* and a collection of letters entitled *The Habit of Being.*

7. *Memento Mori,* by Muriel Spark. This novel, set in London in the 1950's, provides a definite reminder of a telling Ash Wednesday phrase, "Remember, you are dust and unto dust you will return." True, each of us must die, and each of Spark's characters hear these words differently, as past experiences are dredged up. In this unpretentious and adroit contemporary literary classic, the dreaded reality of old age becomes a palpable reality.

8. *Silence,* by Shusaku Endo. I once had the privilege of awarding the Campion Medal, given by the Catholic Book Club, to Mr. Endo. His works, including *The Sea and Poison, Wonderful Fool, Volcano, When I Whistle, The Samurai, Stained Glass Elegies,* and *Scandal,* are well known and deeply appreciated both in his native Japan and throughout the world. In *Silence,* a young missionary, Rodrigues, travels to Japan to investigate rumors that his former teacher, Ferreira, has not only converted to Buddhism but has been participating in the persecution of Christians. Endo's Roman Catholic heritage has charged his artistic sensibilities with a vision and power rarely seen in contemporary writers of whatever nationality.

9. *Mariette in Ecstasy,* by Ron Hansen. The Gerard Manley Hopkins Professor of Literature at Santa Clara University in California, Hansen has built up a loyal following. *Mariette in Ecstasy,* his third novel, focuses on the trials of a young stigmatic, Mariette Baptiste, during her six months in her Upstate New York convent the early part of the 20th century. Hansen is keenly attuned to the give-and-take of convent life, especially the need for human and divine affection among professedly religious women.

10. *Beloved,* by Toni Morrison. I list this novel by Nobel Prize–laureate, Princeton University professor Toni Morrison, not only because it is a marvelous, though sometimes opaque, story of three generations of women (Baby Suggs, Sethe, and Denver) living in Ohio after the Civil War, but because Ms. Morrison once mentioned to me over dinner in Paris that she had been raised a Roman Catholic (I never pursued the topic). Morrison confronts directly the ravages—physical, psychological, and spiritual—that have resulted from slavery, something not lost in the film version of this novel.

Patrick Samway, S.J., former literary editor of *America,* is author of the acclaimed biography *Walker Percy: A Life.*

❧

The Ten Best Catholic Movies You'll Ever See
BY MICHAEL LEACH

1. *A Man for All Seasons.* Paul Scofield is Sir Thomas More, the sixteenth-century saint who gave up his life rather than surrender his conscience. More teaches us not only how to live but how to die. He goes to his death forgiving those who persecuted him and hoping to see them again in heaven. "Be not afraid," he tells his executioner, "you send me to God."

2. *La Strada.* Anthony Quinn is Zampano: an "animal" whose soul comes to life when an innocent (Giulietta Masina) who loves him unconditionally dies for his sins. "Even a stone has a purpose," says a circus clown to the innocent girl. And she, and we, realize that Zampano—and all of us—are as worthy of love and glory as the stars that light Fellini's night.

"Even a stone has a purpose."—*La Strada*

3. *On the Waterfront.* What a story of sin, forgiveness, and redemption! And who can forget Father Barry's (Karl Malden's) *corpus Christi* speech on the docks: "Christ is always with you . . . Christ is in the shapeup. He's on the hatch. He's in the union hall. He's kneeling here beside Nolan." Marlon Brando takes up a cross and proves that it's better to save one's soul than gain a piece of the world.

4. *Going My Way.* Father Bing Crosby and Sister Ingrid Bergman inspired more than one generation of Catholic boys and girls to become priests and nuns. They may not make them like those two anymore, and perhaps they never did, but it's great to have role models.

5. *The Nun's Story.* Audrey Hepburn, aka Holly Golightly, dons a habit and goes to the Dark Continent to serve the sick. A story of conscience, it is the flip side of *Going My Way* as Sister Audrey, in the end, goes her way. Near the end of her career, the shimmering actress would play an angel in Steven Spielberg's *Always*.

6. *Amadeus.* An epic story of two souls: Mozart, a man whose talent came from heaven, and Salieri, a man whose envy put him in hell. A cautionary tale for anyone inclined to envy, and one that teaches that God's grace falls on the just and the unjust alike, or as Clint Eastwood put it to Gene Hackman in *Unforgiven:* "Deservin's got nothing to do with it."

7. *The Mission.* A great conversion story set in South America during the early missionary days. Robert De Niro sheds his armor and gives his life to God. "He who loses his life for my sake shall find it, and he who finds it shall lose it." Both tragic and inspiring, *The Mission* is based on historical events.

8. *Boys Town.* Spencer Tracy is Father Flanagan, the founder of Boys Town, and Mickey Rooney is one of the first of thousands of children to benefit from his inspired idea. Tracy in a memorable scene slaps a cigarette out of Mickey's mouth, but Mickey has the last word: "He ain't heavy, Father. He's my brother." We dare you not to cry.

9. *The Song of Bernadette.* Jennifer Jones shines as the French peasant girl who saw "a beautiful lady" in the town dump, and whose vision casts a glow in the lives of those around her. The miracle is not only what she saw but that she saw. Catholicism is about being open to beauty in the most unlikely places.

10. *The Passion of Joan of Arc.* Carl Dreyer's 1928 classic tells the story of a soul on fire largely through close-ups of her face. Jean Cocteau described the film as looking like "an historical document from an era in which the cinema didn't exist." Silent magic!

Honorable Mentions

The Bells of St. Mary's. This sequel to *Going My Way* could be called *Fr. Rambo/Sr. Rocky II.* Ingrid teaches a boy to box, Bing sings "Ave Maria," and both inspire a millionaire to buy a new school. Perhaps not as sweet as the original but still a lullaby of a movie that cradle-Catholics remember with love.

The Shoes of the Fisherman. Anthony Quinn as Zorba the Pope pledges the church's wealth to the poor, and begs "the great of the world and the small of the world to share their abundance with those who have nothing." Based on a novel by Morris West, the movie moves slowly but quickens the heart with a great Catholic idea.

The Godfather, I and II. Da dada dah' da dah' da. The classic "family" saga and a cautionary tale for anyone who sees religion only as rituals that mark life's milestones. Al Pacino's face at the end of *II* reveals the wages of sin more than any other image in film.

Mean Streets. You can't be Catholic without feeling guilty. You probably can't be alive without feeling guilty. But Martin Scorsese's neighborhood saga is lit with votive candles and casts a small glow on a hard lesson: we are saved not alone but with each other.

ET: The Extra-Terrestrial. Sure, Spielberg is Jewish. But so was Jesus. And any movie that has a dead flower come back to life while a Christ-figure rises from the dead has our vote. "Be good." "I'll be right here." Thank you, Steven, for lifting our spirits as high as the moon!

❧

The Best Catholic Music You'll Ever Hear
BY THOMAS DAY

The musical tradition of the universal Church is a treasure of im-measurable value, greater even than that of any other art. . . . The treasure of sacred music is to be preserved and fostered with very great care.

—Constitution on the Sacred Liturgy,
Vatican Council II

Good news! What Vatican II called Roman Catholicism's "treasure of sacred music"—a remarkable assortment of liturgical music from the Middle Ages to the present—is alive and thriving. Go to the stores that sell recordings; go to the concert halls, colleges, and universities that have choruses, and some churches (in the United States, mostly churches that are Episcopalian and Lutheran). There you will find the Catholic Church's glorious treasure of liturgical music preserved and lovingly fostered.

When this music seems to come out of the community—out of its aspiration and best efforts—this "treasure" is joyous celebration, with congregational participation that is almost hot to the touch . . . and it's fun, too! (When it seems to come from other people "doing their own thing," it can be a great bore.) Composed with human nature in mind, this music has an egalitarian way of reaching out to prince and peasant, male and female. It profoundly communicates with that part of our souls where facts and logic end and wordless communication begins. Perhaps this is what is meant by the sublime and the sublime is, if anything, fun.

MONASTIC
CHOIR OF
ST PETER'S
ABBEY,
SOLESMES

S.838

GREGORIAN
ANTHOLOGY
Following the Rhythm of the Liturgy

GREGORIAN CHANT   *Directed by Dom Jean Claire*

Of course, there are the usual complaints, grumbling, and even expressions of indignation about this music. It is supposedly obsolete, elitist, too difficult for parishes, too expensive, impractical for modern worship, a poisonous influence, "going back," treason against Vatican II, etc. So many dire warnings—and all of them are valid and not valid, wise and silly, perceptive and paranoid, all at the same time. The reality is this: If you are a Catholic, this liturgical music belongs to you; it teaches you something about your faith, something that could never be captured in a hundred sermons. Whether or not it belongs in the local parish is settled on a case-by-case basis.

Starting in the Renaissance, most of this "treasure music" has been composed by members of the laity. The clergy may have held the monopoly on theological truth, but lay composers (many of them wrestling with their own deep and personal experience of sinfulness) could produce a musical interpretation of theological truth that goes beyond the careful formulations of the theologians, beyond the obsessive clarifications of some liturgists.

1. *The entire repertory of Gregorian chant,* with a special affectionate mention of the *Requiem aeternam,* the Introit from the old Gregorian chant *Requiem.* (This *Requiem aeternam* was beautifully sung by a choir at the funeral Mass for Jacqueline Kennedy Onassis.) Some available recordings: anything recorded by the monks of Solesmes Abbey in France since the 1970s (distributed in the United States by Paraclete Press); *Chant,* the bestseller recording by the Benedictine monks of Santo Domingo de Silos; and *Women in Chant* (Sounds True recordings) by the Benedictine nuns of the Abbey of Regina Laudis in Connecticut.

2. *Renaissance Polyphony* by Josquin des Prez (or Pres), Palestrina, William Byrd, and a long list of other composers from about 1450 to 1625. There are some excellent recordings by the following "groups": Chanticleer, the Tallis Scholars, the choir of Kings College (Cambridge), and the choir of the Roman Catholic Westminster Cathedral (London).

3. *The Lord Nelson Mass (Missa in angustiis)* by Franz Joseph Haydn. God smiles and Haydn's liturgical music smiles, too.

4. *Ave Verum Corpus* by Mozart. If this list could be extended, I would include the Masses that Mozart composed (e.g., the *Coronation Mass*).

5. *Mass in C Major, Opus 86,* by Beethoven.

6. *Deutsche Messe* by Franz Schubert, also known as the *German Mass.* This was originally intended as music for the congregation—songs in German to be sung during the Low Mass. Richard Proulx has made a beautiful adaptation of this Mass for the English text (GIA publications). *The Lord, Have Mercy* and *Holy, Holy* are in one widely used Catholic song book; any congregation that knows English could sing this music.

7. *Mass in F Minor* by Anton Bruckner. The best place for this grand statement by Bruckner is the concert hall or the sacred concert given in a church, not the liturgy. His *Mass in E Minor* deserves an honorary place on this list.

8. *Requiem* by Gabriel Fauré. Heaven and earth touch during the instrumental introduction to the Agnus Dei.

9. *Quatre motets pour un temps de pénitence* and *Quatre motets pour le temps de Noël* by Francis Poulenc. The critics usually rely on "un" words like "unassuming" and "unpretentious" to describe this music. Probably a better—and more Catholic—description would be "a deep faith expressed in musical simplicity." The Latin motets in these collections— like some of Poulenc's non-liturgical works, such as the *Gloria* and his *Organ Concerto*—contain an innocence and playfulness that are sometimes banished when composers try to get terribly serious about religion.

10. *La Nativité du Seigneur* by Olivier Messiaen. Speaking in tongues (musical version), the dark night of the soul emerging into the light (the blinding light), fear and trembling, Awake and sing!—it's all here in this organ music by Messiaen. Not everyone will appreciate his mysticism, expressed in dissonance that could strip a coat of paint off the walls, but, what joy! What sheer released energy! And also, what anxiety! Messiaen's *Quartet for the End of Time* is not liturgical music (and, therefore, not in the "treasure of sacred music") but it nevertheless deserves to be included among the writings of the Fathers and Doctors of the Church.

Thomas Day is professor of music at Salve Regina University in Newport, Rhode Island. He is the author of *Where Have You Gone, Michelangelo?* and *Why Catholics Can't Sing*.

❧

Catholic identity is discovered when spirit and soul come together—when human experience is engaged and heart matters, but it's tied into a bigger story, a tradition that gives individual stories universal meaning. That's great religion.

—Richard Rohr, O.F.M.,
author and retreat master
Albuquerque, New Mexico

A Catholic novelist has a vocation, like the priest or apostle. The novel is almost exclusively a creature of Christendom.

—Walker Percy, novelist

You've read *Sacred Clowns*? The people out at St. Bonaventure . . . that's the church. Those guys driving the water trucks, feeding, taking food out to those starving old people. The Little Sisters of the Poor, taking care of those old people in Gallup. That's the church, right there. And the Franciscans at Window Rock, that's the church.

—Tony Hillerman, novelist

The Church's DNA is all over the place.

Being Catholic is a way of looking at the world. It isn't simply church. It's music and art and architecture and literature and philosophy. It's a language all its own. Good God, it's even food and drink.

It's also community. I go to Mass to be with people. I never tire of watching them go to the altar to receive the Eucharist.

It's a messy church. Filled with faults because it is filled with people. It's a church that often puts barbed wire around its own charisms. But, as James Joyce said, being Catholic means "Here comes everybody!"

I love that.

—R. Timothy Unsworth,
columnist and author
Chicago, Illinois

What do these four men have in common?

You're right on both counts.

What about these people?

You're right again.

I am not inclined toward revolution, and Catholicism has given me that minimum of rebellion, maybe a little impish, that rescues me.

—Federico Fellini, film director

I like being Catholic in probably the same way someone else might answer why they like being Christian, or Buddhist, or Muslim, or Jewish. I like it because it has been the way I and countless ancestors of mine have chosen as our method of becoming one with our Creator, and to hopefully follow its rules and tenets to help guide us toward a charitable and joyous life.

—Joe Mantegna, actor

I never wavered. It is the best thing that could have happened to me—to be born Catholic. It gave me a belief in God and the knowledge that God will always take care of me.

—Maureen O'Hara, actress

Playing the role of Peter Maurin was an opportunity to give back to the Catholic Worker what they had given to me. When I was a struggling actor in New York, I used to go to the Catholic Worker house on Spring Street to get free meals—and also food for the soul!

—Martin Sheen, actor

Growing up Catholic has been a gift. Being in the movie business is hard. There are a lot of battles to face, and if I didn't have that religious core—that base to turn to—I would be truly lost.

At times, I see other people who seem adrift because they don't have a spiritual anchor.

—Moira Kelly, actress

Having a faith made a big difference to me. I found out you don't have to get all wound up in religion, but the knowledge that it is there, with its rules and its vast storehouse of experience, gives you an inner security.

—Gary Cooper, actor

Chapter Twelve

HERE COMES EVERYBODY!

Catholicism is not an exclusive club. Mother Teresa was Catholic, and so was Frank Sinatra. I like being Catholic because we don't all have to agree on everything; in fact, we can disagree on plenty, and we can come at being Catholic from all kinds of directions, yet we are all Catholics. James Joyce, no perfect Catholic himself, said it well when he described Catholicism in this way: "Here comes everybody."

—Mitch Finley, author and journalist
Spokane, Washington

I like being a Catholic because it unites me with every other human being on the face of the earth in a deeply personal way.
—Martin Sheen, actor

I like being part of something that has thrown up so many eccentric and remarkable people.

> —Rosemary Haughton,
> theologian and author
> Gloucester, Massachusetts

The most amazing thing about being Catholic to me is that I am
able to unite myself in faith with men and women not only
throughout the world, but throughout the centuries.

> —John Cardinal O'Connor, Archbishop
> New York, New York

ༀ

At Home in Noah's Ark

BY CYPRIAN DAVIS

As a youngster I devoured history books. There I encountered the
Catholic Church with its medieval popes, bishops, saints, and sinners.
When I was in my teens, I became a Catholic. Much later I had less ro-
mantic notions about the church. As an African American, I began to appreciate the church because it was *catholic*, that is universal. Living in a
segregated world alive with racial tension and racial hatred, I saw that the
churches were segregated and often hostile to blacks and other minorities.
Catholicism claimed that everyone was at home in the Catholic Church.
When I looked at the world, despite the racism of some Catholics and
even the segregation of many Catholic churches in the United States, I saw
that men and women of diverse races were completely at home within the
church. I learned about black saints, African popes, and monasticism with
its roots in Africa.

Today I am a monk and still enthralled by the Catholic Church. I love
the beauty of its liturgy in all its rich variety. I love the richness of Catholic
spirituality in all its diversity. I love the fact that the Catholic Church can
be at one and the same time authoritative in its teaching and deeply hu-

manitarian in its social consciousness. There is room for all kinds of
people in the Catholic Church;
some may only be on the fringe,
yet none of us are strangers. No
place is foreign to the Church's
presence. Catholicism has put
down roots in every culture and in
almost every land.

All find their home in the
Catholic Church, and the
Catholic Church is at home with
every people. But this breadth and
inclusiveness does not only mean
universality of race and culture, it
also means that the church is the
meeting place of saints and sinners. It is not an elite corps of the elect but
a large unwieldy ship like Noah's ark with all kinds of people crammed in
the hold trying to make it to port. Universality includes all time. Catholic
means encompassing all time. The church is old and new, ancient and
modern, including all times just as it includes all people.

Cyprian Davis, O.S.B., is a professor of church history at St. Meinrad's
School of Theology in St. Meinrad, Indiana.

❧

Confessions of a Cafeteria Catholic
BY MICHAEL LEACH

It happened in the last century. I had written an essay for *America* magazine called "The Last Catholics in America." Its purpose was to bring
those Catholics who welcome change and those who don't closer together.
The ink had hardly dried when I found myself on a TV talk show with an
executive from Catholics United for the Faith.

CUF is an organization with a profound loyalty to the Pope and the official teachings of the church. Its representative was a middle-age fellow not unlike myself, rumpled from a day of work and no more intimidating than Robert Young in *Father Knows Best.*

While a makeup artist powder-puffed our faces and an electrician wired us for sound, my new friend and I chatted about our jobs and families, and discovered how much we had in common. The only remark he made that frightened me was that he been a guest on *Geraldo.*

The show began. The Man from CUF was cast as the conservative; I was the liberal. That made me nervous because I like to think of myself as a reconciler. My friends at work will tell you that my fiercest ideology is, "Please, let's not argue."

Questions rained on us, and we protected each other with a shared umbrella of civility while answering as best—and cleverly—as we could. At one point, however, my colleague suggested that I was a "Supermarket Catholic," one who picks and chooses pieces of his faith as if it were food rather than follows the current menu of the official church. His choice of phrase inspired a sound bite that went something like this:

"What's so bad about that?" I answered. "The Catholic Church is one of the greatest spiritual supermarkets the world has ever known! It has aisles that never end and its spiritual fruits alone are enough to nourish a person for eternity—not to mention the meat, potatoes, and vegetables. No one can eat everything at once. The problem is that the church has been promoting only a small portion of what is available in its storehouse, and a lot of people are hungry for what's been hidden, including its infinite variety of desserts!"

Showy, sure, but my friend had his sound bites too, and besides, he asked for it. Truth was, we were in a game, and while neither of us meant to hurt the other, to score points (and to our later regret), perhaps we did.

A couple of years later the term Supermarket Catholic devolved into Cafeteria Catholic, a derogatory term used to divide allegedly picky Catholics from those who eat what is put on their plates. The label entered the national consciousness and suddenly the words dissent and assent became dog tags; many Catholics issued zingers on talk shows that played out only in their minds.

Truth is, their Catholic cholesterol levels on the hot issues of the day could never be high enough to separate them from the love of Christ that beat in their hearts. The bloodstream of every Catholic—liberal, conservative, or confused—traces back to the same pool of blood at the foot of a cross.

My television guest and I shared the same spiritual DNA. If we hadn't been playing characters in a game, we would have trumpeted the truth that in reality we were guests at a Great Feast whose tables are set for everyone: "the poor, the crippled, the blind, and the lame . . . and there is still room for more" (Luke 14: 15–24).

Catholicism means throwing a party for everyone. We need someone to remind us: The church is not a country club; it's a family. Dissent doesn't kill families; disinterest does. Cafeteria Catholicism is family talk; Country Club Catholicism is refusing the invitation to a feast prepared for us all.

The church as family fills its tables to bursting for prodigal sons and daughters—morning, noon, and night. Like the parent in that parable, such a church refuses to condemn or even compare one family member to another. It takes Jesus' words to heart: "Judge not so that you might not be judged." Or better yet, "My child, you are always here with me, and everything I have is yours" (Luke 15:31).

The Catholic Church truly is one of the richest spiritual supermarkets the world has ever known. And no one can eat everything at once. But every once in a while, every one of us Catholics needs to remember the invitation of Jesus to a full house, and to cultivate good manners at the table built for us all.

After the TV interview, my colleague and I shook hands, thanked each other for our endeavors to shed light not heat, and resumed our small talk. We didn't say it but we knew that he was as much a Supermarket Catholic as I was, and I was as much a *Prix Fixe* Catholic as he was. Each of us chose to emphasize some parts of our faith over others, but both of us shared the same faith and knew we still had more to learn. The "faith that passes all understanding" is by definition a faith that is always "in search of understanding."

I also knew that the Man from CUF was a good guy who'd be nice to have over for dinner. It didn't happen but only for the same reasons that middle-aged folk seldom have even old friends over for dinner anymore. They talk about it when they bump into each other at the supermarket. They just don't get around to it.

Nobody's perfect.

But after all, who else is the Great Feast for?

❧

In essentials, unity; in doubtful matters, liberty; in all things, charity.

—Pope John XXIII, *Ad Petri Cathedram*

Speaking to the young man who unjustly accused him of a crime, Joseph Cardinal Bernardin forgave him, and said: "We cannot run away from our family. We have only one family, so we must make every effort to be reconciled."

As Catholics, everybody has kind of a shared experience, there is a bond there.

—Leon Panetta, former White House
chief of staff Washington, D.C.

I like being Catholic because it is my home and family. I can walk into a church anywhere and feel at home. After all, my family built them!

I may not agree with every nuance of everything the pope or the priest says, but I'll stick up for him, because he is part of my family. Some family members have their own take on life but we love and accept them anyway, because they're family.

—Mary Ryan-Hotchkiss, chemist
Portland, Oregon

I'm being confirmed Catholic at Easter Vigil Mass this year. A colleague of mine asked me why I wanted to become Catholic and the only reason that I have is: *because there is room.* There is room for me in the Catholic Church, and not just me, for you too, and for my husband's mother who was inspired by devotion to Mary, and for my friend who will probably leave the priesthood because he is gay but remains Catholic, and for my other friend who used to worry about unbaptized babies going to limbo but doesn't worry about that anymore, and for Richard Rohr who is very critical of the way the authorities in the church practice what they preach about social justice, and for Anthony DeMello even though his teachings are questioned, and for the Pope. It's kind of like asking why Jesus was born in that particular manger. I guess the answer is because there was room for him and his family there. It wasn't a palace and neither is the Catholic Church. It was not the only manger in town or even the one with the best accommodations, probably. But when you are aching to be born, wherever there is room for you and your family will do just fine.

— Tammy Greer
Picayune, Mississippi

Did you hear about the three priests who were discussing the problems they had been having with bats in the bell towers of their churches?

"I tried clanging garbage cans together and playing loud music," said the first priest, "but the bats left for a few hours and then returned."

"I actually shot off fireworks in the bell tower," said the second priest, "but the bats went away for a few days and then returned."

"Well, I solved the problem permanently," said the third priest.

"What did you do?" the other two asked him.

"I just baptized and confirmed the bats and they never came back to church again," he said.

The thing I like about Catholicism is that someone could tell that story to a roomful of lay people and get as big laugh as would come from any group of frustrated priests or religious. A church that can laugh at itself is all right in my book.

Our ability to poke fun at our failings and foibles as a people of faith is, to my mind, one of the best things about being Catholic.

—Gregory F. Augustine Pierce, publisher
Chicago, Illinois

I like being Catholic because we have a big tradition—2000 years worth. And we're big in the sense that we're international. When parish life seems mired in less positive aspects of American culture or seems just too, well . . . parochial, I like to remember the Venezuelan village I lived in for two years and what it was like to be Catholic there. Or I think of the African villages where our diocese has a team of missioners. And I remember how much bigger the church is, indeed how much bigger God is, than any of this.

The Catholic Church is also big in the sense that there's room for everybody. Of course, there are always voices within the church rejecting the unorthodox or rejecting a musty theology— or rejecting any number of things in between. But here we all are standing shoulder to shoulder on Sunday and shuffling down the aisle to receive the Eucharist because we know how much we need it. We're contentious, but we're all Catholics.

—Carol Schuck Scheiber,
public relations consultant
Toledo, Ohio

I like being a Catholic because of its rich, diverse, and one can say even, at times, perverse history. As a convert to Catholicism, I questioned initially my calling but came to realize that at this time and place I could not be other than Catholic. Being Catholic provides me with a constant challenge to my faith as I struggle with issues considered too inflammatory but which, as a lay Black woman, I find absolutely essential to engage in dialogue about. I see it as vital that the full history of the church be explored and exposed and that it is part of my task as a Catholic to be engaged in the act of so exploring and exposing in order to uncover the layers hidden so long and to set them forth for all to see. I like being a Catholic because, unlike when I was a Methodist attorney, as a Catholic theologian I have never been bored!

—Diana L. Hayes, professor of theology
(Georgetown University)
Washington, D.C.

Catholicism is not a perfectionistic sect allowing only the saints and the perfect to dwell. It is a people on an individual and social pilgrimage pointed toward a perfection not yet achieved. The Catholic Church is never any better or worse than the local congregation, which is its actual realization. In every parish there are decent people, a few saints, many ordinary folks, and a minority of real rotters. That is the church since *church* in the abstract is just that—an abstraction. The very complexity of the tradition indicates that within this tradition there should be something for everyone. When we find that *something*, we might also encounter the *Someone* who stands at the heart of this long, messy, and complex reality called the Catholic Church.

—Lawrence S. Cunningham,
professor of theology (Notre Dame)
Notre Dame, Indiana

When we call ourselves Catholic, what we're saying is that God has invited us into the human struggle and the church is the place of that struggle. The church isn't a place where the converted gather; the church is the place where conversion happens. It is the place where one is forced to see the complexities, idiosyncrasies, and brokenness of humanity.

—Richard Rohr, O.F.M.,
author and retreat director
Albuquerque, New Mexico

HERE COMES EVERYBODY!
PHOTO GALLERY

"Catholicism means 'Here Comes Everybody.'"
—James Joyce

Row 1: Pope John Paul II, Pope John XXIII, Pope Pius XII
Row 2: Mother Teresa, Mother Seton, Sara Leach (Mike's mom)
Row 3: Ethel Waters, Grace Kelly, Sophia Loren

Row 4: John Wayne, Arnold Schwarzenegger, Mel Gibson
Row 5: Michelangelo, Sister Wendy Beckett, Andy Warhol
Row 6: Maria von Trapp, Sister Thea Bowman, Susan Sarandon

Row 7: Fulton Sheen, Martin Sheen, Charlie Sheen
Row 8: Alfred Hitchcock, Martin Scorsese, Federico Fellini
Row 9: Oscar Romero, Jean Donovan, John F. Kennedy

INTERLUDE

It has taken me nearly thirty years (my whole life) to say, "I like being Catholic." Truth is, I love it. But my faith journey has been a slow, winding path toward developing "eyes to see" and "ears to hear" God at work in my life and in the world. These "God moments," as I call them, are part of each of our lives, but it is in and through and with the church that I become a skilled enough observer to recognize and act on them. Mass, parish functions, Bible study, conversations with my peers and our faith community, graduate school, publishing, and social service are my classrooms and teachers.

For me, and for many young adults, the beauty of the church is not that it offers rigid answers but that it embraces and provokes profound questions. Not that it assesses sin, blame, and punishment but that it calls for integration, reconciliation, and accountability. Not that it excludes and divides but includes and unites. Not that it fights for a fragile future as an institution but that it fights to be the body of Christ on earth. I knew I loved being Catholic the day I realized that the church is built on the foundation not of perfect people but of passionate seekers like Jesus, Saint Augustine, Thérèse of Lisieux, Thomas Merton, Dorothy Day. For the church's vitality comes from all of us seekers whose restless hearts beat furiously in the name of God's peace, justice, and love until they finally return home to the Source from which they came.

—Jeremy Langford, twenty-nine years old,
editor, Chicago, Illinois

As a Roman Catholic, I feel I witness God's compassion for my family and others.

—Marc Munfakh, sixteen years old
Manhasset, New York

I like being Catholic because Catholicism mentored me in accepting myself and others as human beings. Catholic theologians taught me to think for human freedom; Catholic activists freed me to act for human dignity; Catholic mystics opened me to contemplate the human mystery. And my Catholic parents encouraged me to own my faith, blessing my spiritual—and quite human—restlessness.

—Tom Beaudoin, thirty years old,
theologian
Atlanta, Georgia

I suppose I like being Catholic the way I "like" having oxygen: I can't imagine life being possible without my faith. It's the vocabulary that makes sense of everything else. Jesus Christ is the center and meaning of history. The Church is His bride. So living the Catholic faith actively, joyfully, evangelically, and leading others to it—these are the most exhilarating things anyone can do with a life.

—Charles J. Chaput, O.F.M. Cap.,
Archbishop
Denver, Colorado

Religion was never oppressive or even conspicuous in our household, but it was always there, part of our lives, and the church's teachings and customs were observed. We went to Mass on Sundays, holy days, First Fridays. We said grace before meals. . . . I would choose a different child each time to say grace. At Sunday dinner after Mass, we generally had a little discussion of what the sermon had been about, what the Gospel message meant, so the children would pay attention during Mass. If it was a holy day or a favorite saint's day, we discussed its meaning and asked what the saint's life could teach us. At Easter, of course, we asked the meaning of the resurrection and life everlasting. . . . Faith, I would tell them, is a great gift from God and is a living gift, to sustain us in our lives on earth, to guide us in our activities, to be a source of solace and comfort, so we should help it grow and flourish, and try never to lose it.

—Rose Fitzgerald Kennedy

ONE CHURCH, TWO ERAS

A Young Adult Catholic Looks Back with Love

BY THERESE J. BORCHARD

A priest friend used to make me stare at a poster he had pinned to his wall. "What do you see?" he'd ask.

"Dots," I'd answer. "Random dots."

"Look closer," he'd challenge me. "Relax your eyes, and tell me what you see."

I'd get so impatient. What was his point? That's wonderful if he sees a praying mantis tickling a gorilla underneath a palm tree, but I have better things to do.

Yet, as luck had it, he was helping me with a school project so I played the game every week. He had made it his mission to help me to see something real in the midst of dots.

Finally on a slow day toward the end of our project, I determined to see what I had not yet been able to see.

At first all I saw was dots.

I relaxed my eyes. Still more dots.

But then my eyes fell on one cluster of dots, and I saw what looked like the hind feather of a parrot. Then the entire parrot. Then a monkey climbing a tree beside the parrot, an alligator crawling beneath them and wild butterflies floating above them.

Suddenly the dots transformed into a beautiful rain forest bursting with color and all kinds of exotic plants and animals.

"Do you see it?" my friend asked. He had to ask again, laughing at the look of wonder on my face.

"Yes," I answered. "Now I see."

This story illustrates my fleeting visions of God, church, and all the rich traditions and rituals that are part of Catholicism. I look back on those moments of vision with love.

Most of the time all I see is dots. Random dots with no apparent order or pattern. Chaos.

But then comes that rare moment when like the blind man in the gospel I can say, "Now I see." It's like seeing a rainbow after heavy rains. It comes out of nowhere to remind me that there is meaning in all of life's random events, that there is a Beauty in the midst of the dots. That moment is what Catholics call grace.

Grace runs through "the chosen part of things" to reassure me that God is alive and well in the world, and that my faith in the church, in tradition, and in God, is not in vain.

Grace explains to me the goodness that comes from tragedy, the union that comes from separation: how something so tragic as the death of my father could bring together a divided family in love.

I also look back with love on sacramentality, another "chosen part" of Catholicism. The church defines sacramentality as a "visible sign of an invisible grace." I look back with love at the signs of love I've found in people, places, and things around me. My husband Eric. Friends. The squirrel scrambling from branch to branch on the tree outside my window.

Sacramentality allows me to see things that I would otherwise ignore or resist, like spotting the parrot in the poster. As a Catholic I look at things differently, whether I like it or not. Catholicism is a way of seeing.

My faith opens my eyes to the good and the beautiful in everything around me. When grace strikes, an apple becomes more than an apple, peanut butter more than one of my favorite foods. Everything that I enjoy in an average day is pregnant with the goodness of God.

It's not that my fruits and vegetables start dancing and singing like they do in a Disney cartoon; it's that the dots become connected and I get a glimpse of what's really there.

Finally, I look back with love, and with gratitude, on incarnation: God's becoming human in each and every one of us. Its meaning for me is embodied in a prayer of St. Francis, which I repeat like a mantra every time I am on an airplane or fear death.

At those moments I abbreviate his classic prayer about peace something like this: "Dear Lord, if I am to die, please let people remember of me only that which was You. Let my life serve merely as a witness to your Love." I understand incarnation as God's becoming human so that we humans can become more like God. Maybe I got the idea from Mother Teresa, who composed this prayer:

> *Dear Jesus,*
> *Help us to spread your fragrance everywhere we go.*
> *Flood our souls with your Spirit and life.*
> *Penetrate and possess our whole being so utterly*
> *that our lives may only be a radiance of yours.*

In the moments between grace—when I fear that I will never see more than dots—I remember "the chosen part of things." I look back with love on the rituals and traditions and spiritual ideas that have sustained my faith for as long as I can recall. And so I also look back with gratitude to loving mentors such as my mother and my grandmother, priests and teachers and friends like Mike Leach, who have generously shared their wisdom with me and my generation so that we can in turn pass on "the chosen part of things" to a younger age.

I like being Catholic because it gives me a new way of seeing, of living, of being. My faith assures me that grace will consistently visit me— accompanied by sacramentality and incarnation—to remind me that life has meaning and that God is always here. As a young adult Catholic I know that there will always be a rain forest or a rainbow in the midst of life's dots. And I know that I'll always look with love upon those who have gone before me and taught me to be interested in seeing what is really there, what is already in my eyes.

❧

An Elder Catholic Looks Forward with Hope
BY MICHAEL LEACH

You're familiar with the fearsome forecasts. The headlines tremble from the front pages. They read something like this:

- Before too long the average age of the parish priest will be 102, and all three of them will be doing baptisms, weddings, and funerals in New York, Chicago, and Los Angeles until they drop.
- Not only is church attendance falling but churches are closing their doors before the average churchgoer can park the car.
- The average American Catholic now gives only 1 percent of his income to the church, and is soon expected to ask for a refund.

You ask yourself: "Am I one of the last Catholics in America?" Well, if you can still hum the melody of "Tantum Ergo," you probably are. But if you're still more interested in the good news than in the gloom-and-doom statistics, you can also look forward to a new century of Catholicism that may be more filled with faith, hope, and charity than any before it.

Signs of new life are everywhere, pushing up like blades of grass through an old highway that leads to a shared destination.

- Young people from all over the world, their spirits higher than the Mile High City, celebrate Eucharist in Denver with a seventy-nine-year-old pope on World Youth Day.
- Eighteen thousand adults and twelve thousand young people—singing and sharing their Catholic faith—shake the rafters of the Anaheim Convention Center, a block away from Disneyland, during the Los Angeles Religious Education Congress.

149

- Busloads of students from 242 colleges and universities in forty-two states join hands with Maryknoll Father Roy Bourgois, actor Martin Sheen, and several thousand other adults who have led the way in a protest calling for the closing of the notorious School of the Americas in Fort Benning, Georgia.
- On warm July evenings in Chicago when many young adults are off to a Cubs game or walking along the lakefront, more than 2,500 of them gather in sixty-three parishes to share and discover their faith with each other and with some of the "last Catholics in America" in the Archdiocese's "Theology on Tap" program.

The last Catholics in America are those of us over fifty, and—like it or not—we represent a last breed in American Catholic culture. That's not something to lament, but to celebrate and share. Few people younger than us have experienced both the old and the new church as we have. We have an opportunity to retrieve what is dearest and freshest in our heritage and pass it along to them in a form that doesn't fracture the past but flows from it. If we hold up what Teilhard de Chardin called "the chosen part of things," the things that last, our children will recognize them, and the church they shape will shine with a beauty that is "ever ancient, ever new."

The "chosen part" is the spiritual reality of things. We feel water running down our forehead at Baptism but in reality it is forgiveness and assurance. We watch a priest or a sister or a layperson handing out wafers but in reality we are seeing God's spiritual child sharing God's spiritual Life with God's spiritual children—and all are somehow mysteriously One. A holy card is not a holy card but a reminder of courage. A march against violence is not a protest but an affirmation of solidarity and justice. And the figure nailed to a cross is not a man on a cross but incredibly—in truth—unbounded Love. Catholicism is all about seeing beyond appearances, and beholding what is really there: truth, love, mercy, goodness, beauty, harmony, compassion, gratitude, peace and joy. These are the "chosen part of things."

We know that words spoken about God are not God, and that the words we read are not the same as the truth that sets us free. The Zen

Master says, "The finger pointing at the moon is not the moon." *A Course in Miracles* says, "Words are symbols of symbols and thus twice removed from reality." *The Catechism of the Catholic Church* says, "We do not believe in formulas, but in the realities they express." And Jesus says, "God is Spirit, and they that worship Him must worship Him in spirit and in truth" (John 4:24).

Words change. Formulas revise. Appearances appear and disappear. But the chosen part, that which lasts, which is spirit, remains forever. Catholicism is about seeing what is really there.

Catholics, like everyone else, behold the "chosen part of things" when they least expect it. The poet Cyrano said:

> *There comes a moment to everyone*
> *when Beauty stands staring into the soul with sad, sweet eyes*
> *that sicken at the sound of words,*
> *and God help those who pass that moment by.*

Every last Catholic in America can recall a moment beyond words when grace came crashing through consciousness and suddenly they could see. A moment for me came in Chicago when I was in my early twenties. I was walking down Clark Street at dusk. I saw an old woman, bent over like a hairpin, bobbing slowly as she walked alongside a wall. A man with whiskers drinking from a small bottle wrapped in a paper bag. A little girl playing jacks on a cracked sidewalk next to an empty lot. A line from a poem by Gerard Manley Hopkins played in my mind:

> *Christ plays in ten thousand places,*
> *Lovely in limbs, lovely in eyes not his,*
> *For the Father through the features of men's faces.*

And suddenly I knew: Each of them wore the face of Christ in a different way. We were all, somehow, the same. The words vanished. I saw what was really there.

It lasted only a moment. But I'll never forget it.

It's no surprise that one of the last Catholics in America at the time had prepared me for that moment. Father Ignatius Burrill, my English teacher, had taught me to love the poetry of Hopkins.

Our rare moments of seeing are surely direct gifts from God; but those who plant the seeds for those moments are precious gifts too. Words are no more than "fingers pointing at the moon," but we need good ones to point us in the right direction. We know the words are reliable only if they "bear good fruit." The church teaches that the fruits of the spirit are "love, joy, peace, patience, kindness, generosity, faithfulness, gentleness, and self-control" (Gal.5). These fruits tell us if we're going in the right direction. The rest is up to God.

Catholic tradition also speaks of the gifts of the Holy Spirit: "wisdom, understanding, counsel, fortitude, knowledge, awe of the Lord, and piety" (Isa. 11:1–3). These gifts come when we least expect them.

As we've seen, many of today's last Catholics in America are joining with a new generation to plant and share fruits of the spirit. And while many elder Catholics are passing on vintage wine from old wineskins, their younger sisters and brothers are helping them to appreciate new wineskins that hold the wine. They are preparing each other to receive the gifts of the Spirit.

Increasingly, Catholics of all ages are climbing into the attic of Christian consciousness and discovering heirlooms long ignored that remind us of who we really are. Many young adult Catholics have polished them on the pages of this book. Their names are Robert E. Murphy, Marc Munfakh, Heidi Schlumpf, Patti Byrns, Eugene Justin Lee, Liz Collier, Trace Murphy, Tom Beaudoin, Jeremy Langford, and my colleague Therese Johnson Borchard who coedited and cowrote *I Like Being Catholic*. They are the future of the church, present now.

And they face their own unique opportunity. Their peers get their information about things Catholic mostly from newspapers and television—which for the most part report only what high-profile church people are saying about controversial issues. The portrait presented is incomplete, like a *Mona Lisa* without a smile or a *Pietà* without an embrace. Tomorrow's last Catholics in America are challenged to look for the things that last, to surface what Hopkins called "the dearest freshness deep down things," and by their lives to lead the world to see what is really there. They don't have to say anything or do anything; they need only be interested in coming to know "God and Jesus Christ whom God has sent" (John 17:3). All the rest will follow.

The church they shape will in some ways look as different from the church of our generation as ours does from the immigrant church of the early twentieth century. That's neither good nor bad, but necessary and inevitable. Appearances always change. The "chosen part," that which comes from God, is always here. There is nothing to fear.

When the final history of the church is written, it may well remind us of a kaleidoscope—that wonderful child's toy that we hold to the light to see beauty and harmony unfold. As the kaleidoscope turns, tiny bits and pieces of colored glass come dashing and crashing to the center to form new and beautiful designs. Each design is new, each is different, but somehow all are the same. The center is Christ, and it is he who draws all things together, and makes them new.

The kaleidoscope keeps turning but the center never changes. It is the same yesterday, today, and tomorrow. To be Catholic is to appreciate change, to look for the One, and to see the face of Christ in everyone.

Catholicism is all about seeing.

What will tomorrow's last Catholics see? It's already shining in their eyes. And it's wonderful.

Michael Leach is the executive director of Orbis Books. A leader in religious book publishing for three decades, he has edited and published more than a thousand books. His authors include Nobel Prize winners, National Book Award winners, and scores of Catholic Book Award winners. He has served as president of both the Catholic Book Publishers Association and the ecumenical Religion Publishers Group. Mike and his wife Vickie have two grown children and live in Connecticut.

Therese Johnson Borchard holds an M.A. degree in theology from the University of Notre Dame and a B.A. in religious studies from Saint Mary's College. She is a widely published author who has specialized in renewing Catholic traditions for a modern audience. Her books include *Our Catholic Devotions, Our Catholic Prayer, Our Blessed Mother*, and an acclaimed series of children's books, The Emerald Bible Collection, featuring *Whitney Rides the Whale with Jonah, Whitney Coaches David on Fighting Goliath,* and *Whitney Stows Away on Noah's Ark.* Therese and her husband Eric live in Maryland.

ACKNOWLEDGMENTS

We are grateful to the writers, artists, and "people in the pews" whose original words shine on the pages of this book, and to the publishers who gave us permission to reprint sparkling excerpts from their books, magazines, and newspapers.

We are particularly grateful to Andrew Greeley, who coined the phrase "I like being Catholic," and who hasn't gotten enough credit for it until now. Thank you, Father Greeley, from all of us!

Our special thanks also go to the following:

- Tom McGrath and Mary Lynn Hendrickson of *U.S. Catholic* for their enthusiastic support as well as for excerpts from their award-winning magazine;
- Tom Lorsung, Anne LeVeque, and Mark Pattison of Catholic News Service for their kindness in helping us find additional quotes from Catholic celebrities;
- Richard Reece of *Catholic Digest* magazine, John Meyer of Liguori Publications, and Penny Sandoval of *Maryknoll* magazine for graciously providing key material;
- The editors of *Catholic Sentinel, Vermont Catholic Tribune, The Catholic Mirror, Catholic Messenger, The Catholic Advocate, Catholic Telegraph, The Long Island Catholic,* and *Catholic Today* for generously running our request for reader contributions in their newspapers;
- Monsignor William Shannon for checking our final draft;
- All the wonderful professionals at Doubleday for turning it into a beautiful book and making it public: Lorraine Hyland, Carol Christiansen,

Trace Murphy, Elizabeth Walter, Angela Baggetta, John Crenshaw, Lisa McCormick, to name a few, and the entire marketing/sales team.

Most of all we are grateful to our editor and publisher, Eric Major, for catching and sharing the vision; to our agent, Joe Durepos, for his unflagging enthusiasm and encouragement; and to our spouses, Vickie Leach and Eric Borchard, for their constant love and support.

P E R M I S S I O N S

The editors have endeavored to credit all known persons holding copyright or reproduction rights for passages quoted and for illustrations reproduced in this book, especially:

The Abbey of Gethsemani Archives, for photograph of Thomas Merton.

America, March 8, 1997, Vol. 176, No. 8, for excerpt from Claire King.

Arte & Immagini srl/Corbis, for image of Michelangelo by Daniele da Volterra.

Bantam Books, a division of Random House, Inc., for excerpt from *A Book of Saints* by Anne Gordon. © 1994 by Anne Gordon.

Bettmann/Corbis, for photograph of Federico Fellini.

Catholic Digest, April 1996, July 1996, September 1996, April 1998, for selected quotes and excerpts.

Catholic News Service, for selected quotes and excerpts from celebrity interviews.

Chicago Cubs, for photograph of Sammy Sosa.

Corbis, for photographs of Andy Warhol and Ethel Waters.

Corbis-Bettman, for photograph of Roger Maris.

The Crossroad Publishing Company, for excerpt from *The Way of Love* by Pope John Paul II. Copyright © 1981, 1995 by Tony Castle.

Doubleday, a division of Random House, Inc., for excerpts from *Nearer My God* by William F. Buckley, Jr. Copyright © 1997 by William F. Buckley, Jr.

Doubleday, a division of Random House, Inc., for excerpts from *Times to Remember* by Rose Fitzgerald Kennedy. Copyright © 1974, 1995 by Rose Fitzgerald Kennedy.

Nicholas Murray, for photograph of Babe Ruth.

Paraclete Press, for CD jacket of *Gregorian Requiem*. Catalog available from Paraclete Press, P.O. Box 1568, Orleans, MA 02653.

Paulist Press, for children's prayer from *Incense, Bells, and Candles* by Susan Heyboer O'Keefe. Copyright © 2001 by Susan Heyboer O'Keefe.

Photo File, for photograph of Mark McGwire.

Random House, Inc., for excerpt from *Diaries of Mario M. Cuomo: The Campaign for Governor* by Mario M. Cuomo. Copyright © 1984 by Mario M. Cuomo.

Rick Reinhard, for photograph of Sister Thea Bowman.

Robert Finkelstein and Ed Thrasher, for photograph of Frank Sinatra.

St. Anthony Messenger, October 1997, Vol. 105, No. 10, and Kathy Coffey, for excerpts from "Ten Good Reasons to Be Catholic." Used by permission of St. Anthony Messenger Press, 1615 Republic St., Cincinnati, OH 45210.

Shooting Stars, for selected photographs of celebrities. Used by permission of Shooting Stars, P. O. Box 1349, Morongo Valley, CA 92256.

Simon & Schuster, Inc., for excerpt from *Wait Till Next Year* by Doris Kearns Goodwin. Copyright © 1997 by Blithedale Productions, Inc.

Stephen Gill, for photograph of Sister Wendy Beckett.

Steve Kagan, for photograph of Joan Wester Anderson.

U.S. Catholic, May 1994, December 1994, July 1997 for selected excerpts.

U.S. News & World Report, Inc., for excerpt from *Letters for Our Children*, edited by Erica Goode and Jeannye Thomton. Copyright © 1996 by U.S. News & World Report, Inc.

Vicki Shuck for illustrations. Available from Vicki Shuck, 1952 N.E. Hollow Tree Lane, Bend, OR 97701.